Peter Sc33

THIS IS *Board Sailing*

UWE FARKE · VOLKER MÖHLE · DETLEF SCHRÖDER

NAUTICAL BOOKS
MACMILLAN

Copyright © Delius Klasing & Co 1982
Copyright © English language translation Macmillan London
Ltd 1984

First published in Great Britain 1984 by NAUTICAL BOOKS
an imprint of Macmillan London Ltd
4 Little Essex Street
London WC2R 3LF

Associated companies throughout the world

Translated by Barbara Webb. All rights reserved.
No part of this publication may be
reproduced or transmitted, in any form or by
any means, without permission.

ISBN 0 333 366948

Typeset by Filmtype Services Ltd, Scarborough
Printed in Germany

Contents

Introduction	5	Roof rack	28	Being towed	52

Introduction — 5

How do I learn to boardsail? — 8
Why take a boardsailing test? — 8
Who can learn to boardsail? — 8

Where do I learn to boardsail? — 10

Boardsailing waters in general — 10
What are the most suitable waters to learn on and to practise on as a beginner? — 11

Nature and the environment — 15

Rules for protecting the environment — 16
Rules for nature conservation — 17

What is a sailboard? — 19

Basic equipment for a beginner — 19

Notes on the rig — 19
Notes on the board — 22
Material — 24
Tools — 24
Spare parts — 24
Buying second-hand — 24
Additional equipment — 26
Clothing — 26

The journey to your sailing area — 28

Permitted load — 28

Roof rack — 28
Anti-theft measures — 29
Loading up the roof rack — 30
Driving with a board on the roof — 31
Have you remembered everything? — 31
From the car park to the water — 32

Assembling the rig — 33

Knots — 34
Rigging — 36
Tuning the sail — 38
Care of your equipment — 39
Checking on board and rig — 41

Unrigging on the water – practised on land — 42

Playing and practising with board and rig — 44

Practising with the board — 44
Practising with board and rig — 45
Games and safety rules for children — 46

Taking the board and rig to the water — 47

Paddling with the sail extended — 49

The way home — 50

International Distress Signal — 51

Being towed — 52

Climbing on to the board — 54

In shallow water — 54
In deep water — 54
Typical faults — 54

Raising the sail – rig to leeward — 56

Important advice — 56

Shifting the sail from windward to leeward before raising it out of the water — 58

Shifting the rig over the board from windward to leeward — 58
Shifting the rig from windward to leeward by turning the board — 60
Common errors when raising the sail — 62

Basic Position – Safety Position — 63

Moving through the water by swinging the rig — 64

The basic position and exercises with the rig preparatory to moving off — 64

180° turn — 66

From raking the rig to the 180° turn — 68

Right of way between craft	71	**Tacking**	104
1. Power gives way to sail	71	**Gybing**	106
2. Muscle power gives way to sail	72	**The wind you sail with**	108
3. Right of way rules when sailing vessels meet	72	**Wind and Weather**	110
Recommendations on how to behave in busy waters	74	Weather forecast	110
		Wind and storm warnings	111
Starting	76	Thunderstorms	112
Practising balancing the rig	78	**Sailing in circles**	114
Preparing to start	80	**When will I be an expert board sailor?**	116
Starting	80		
Waiting position	80	**Where do I go from here?**	118
Starting position	83	Racing	118
Starting	84	Freestyle	119
Emergency Stop	86	Sailing in surf	119
Points of sailing	88	**Index**	120
Altering course – how to steer	90		
Steering in practice	92		
Luffing up	93		
Bearing away	93		
Bad steering causes catapulting	94		
The theory of steering	95		
How does the sail work?	97		
The importance of sail camber	97		
The importance of the angle of attack	97		
Airflow over the sail	98		
Blanketing, wind shadow	99		
Lateral force and driving force	100		
Tacking and gybing	102		
Tacking	102		
Gybing	103		

Introduction

Was your interest in boardsailing awakened as a result of watching people sailing, perhaps as you walked by a small lake or reservoir? Or did you see them when you were holidaying at the coast or in the Mediterranean, or possibly on television? All that you will have seen and heard of boardsailing will have convinced you that it is a very wet pastime – a sport that involves many a ducking. This is largely true, of course. In the learning stages, boardsailing is a very wet sport indeed, but this is a problem that you soon get over. Given the right instructions you find that you start falling in less frequently even during your first lesson and, at the latest, after just one summer's boardsailing you will feel almost as much at home on a board as on dry land. Difficulties

Even good boardsailors fall in.

only arise again much later when you decide that you are dissatisfied with sailing in light breezes and calm water. Even though physical control and fitness improve with practice, it takes a great deal more practice and experience before you can cope with the extreme demands made, for example, when sailing in surf, when making use of waves to lift the board and jump, or when doing complicated freestyle tricks. You gradually gain the confidence to go out in stronger winds and in waves, and find that you become more and more sure – but however well you manage to sail in the future, an occasional fall into the water will be as inevitable for you as for other boardsailors.

Someone who has decided to learn how to boardsail will find that this book gives practical instruction, while a person who has already made a start and is asking 'How can I improve?' will find here the answers to many of the questions and problems that are bothering him.

The method described in this book has many advantages over older methods of instruction, and correct technique will enable you to move smoothly on to all variations of boardsailing. The new technique that you will learn here is essentially similar to the style which has been developed by, and is typical of, those who have performed best in the last few years, and it differs considerably from the 'old' style. Characteristic of the new technique is the fact that less effort is expended because of the upright, and therefore more relaxed,

Wrong: you should not look like this.

stance, while even beginners can see clearly how easy the movements are.

Boardsailing is a type of sport which depends on technique, equipment and the environment, and you therefore need to know something about the way the gear functions as well as about the wind and the water. Even though this book is intended primarily as an accompaniment to practical work, theoretical questions are not ignored but are tackled at the appropriate moment, when theory is needed in order to understand and supplement practical sailing skills. Photographs showing how not to do it should help you to avoid typical beginners' mistakes.

When engaged in the sport of boardsailing, you have to consider other people; there are other sailors, of course, and people taking part in various water sports – swimmers, fishermen and holidaymakers in pedalos; naturally, there is commercial shipping as well. Last, but not least, boardsailing is an open air sport, pursued in natural surroundings, and you are therefore responsible for caring for the environment, and for protecting and preserving nature.

Once you have worked right through this book thoroughly and have also absorbed the theoretical sections, you will be ready to test your ability, perhaps by taking national tests, and able to enjoy improving all the time.

Now, let's make a start; have fun!

Modern style.

How do I learn to boardsail?

You will have most fun while learning to boardsail if you start off in company, say with your family, with a close friend, or with those in your circle of friends who are like-minded. You can check immediately how well you are doing and how much you know if you sail as a twosome or in a small group, and you will not only benefit from mutual help and support and from each other's successes but will learn from each other's mistakes. When you practise alone it is possible to keep on doing the same action in a sequence of actions wrong, for example, the actual starting action when getting under way, and to keep falling in for that reason. Sometimes you cannot find out for yourself what your mistake is, and it is then a great help if someone else, who has spotted the mistake, makes a suggestion and corrects you. Examples of typical mistakes of this sort should also help you, and, in this book, photographs showing wrong actions accompany those showing the right way to do it. You can, of course, also go to a boardsailing school where instruction is usually in small groups. Your instructor will set you specific exercises to match your ability, and will instruct and correct you.

Why take a boardsailing test?

Whether you learn to boardsail by having lessons from an instructor or by teaching yourself, you should consider whether to take a test which will provide you with a certificate that proves you are able to boardsail. Fortunately there are very few waters where such a certificate is obligatory, but this state of affairs could change rapidly. Obtaining a certificate of this sort voluntarily could forestall the need for official regulations.

Proof that you have passed a windsurfing test is generally required if you want to hire equipment when on holiday or away for a weekend. Generally you will be unable to hire gear unless you have some proof of your theoretical and practical ability. A test like this also serves to convince you of your own ability, so that you prove to yourself that you can control your board without endangering yourself or other people.

Who can learn to boardsail?

There is one absolutely essential requirement if you are to learn to boardsail – you must be able to swim, and that means to be able to swim for a good quarter of an hour when out of your depth. Falling in unintentionally (and possibly getting your head under water for a few moments) is part and parcel of boardsailing – especially when you are at the learning stage. Life-jackets and buoyancy aids of all sorts are available, of course, and your board is unsinkable and therefore a 'life raft' when things become really difficult but, particularly when sailing in waves or strong winds, you can find yourself in the water some distance away from your drifting board, and that poses problems if you are a weak swimmer. Last but not least, you should be so much at home in the water that you can stand by others if need be.

It can be said in general that (almost) anybody can learn to boardsail, given correct instruction. As a slogan you might say 'Boardsailing is a sport for 7- to 70-year-olds', but there are some restrictions. With children under 12 years or so, you have to take into account how far the individual has developed physically. In most cases, the children themselves know their physical limitations and what they can do. When too much is demanded of them, they will not enjoy a sport, and this is particularly true of boardsailing.

Much the same goes for older people; they themselves will know what they want to do and what they are able to do. Broadly speaking, it takes rather longer for older people to feel at home on a sailboard – but no other restrictions need to be made in their case. On the contrary, boardsailing can provide older people with exercise and relaxation.

As far as health and boardsailing goes, there are only a few restrictions that have to be made. If you suffer from rheumatic trouble, or a slipped disc, you must ask your doctor before taking up boardsailing. As is true of other types of water sports, your eardrums must be undamaged because water penetrating your eardrums when you swim or become submerged can upset your balancing organs.

If you suffer from heart or circulation problems, and particularly from high blood pressure, avoid risking your health and do not boardsail unless, after an examination, your doctor has specifically given you permission.

The group rest and talk shop.

Where do I learn to boardsail?

Boardsailing waters in general

You do not need a lavish marina or a permanent mooring if you take up boardsailing. Your equipment can be carried on the roof of a car without difficulty, and it can be assembled and dismantled easily and quickly. The ideal is to find a place where you can park fairly close to the water, or where there is access to the water with a place right by the shore where you can put down the board to rig and unrig it. Any patch of water is suitable, therefore, provided that water sports are permitted, and swimming and boardsailing are not expressly forbidden.

You can normally assume that waters may be used for boardsailing if you can see sailors or boardsailors out there already, but it may well be that certain conditions have to be met, such as paying a fee for sailing there; again the water may only be open at certain times, access may be limited, or you may have to stay a minimum or maximum distance from the bank or shore. Part of the foreshore, the water itself or some of the land near the water could be a nature reserve (see Nature and the Environment p. 15). Occasionally zones are reserved for special types of sport, such as water-skiing, and may not be used for other purposes.

> Boardsailing is generally not allowed where zones are marked for swimming, nor near ship and boat moorings and in harbours, nor in port and harbour entrances and exits.

It is essential to find out whether there are restrictions, and what they are before you decide to boardsail in particular waters. You will find reliable information on signs and notices which tell you what you may or may not do, or you can ask the officials responsible, or the owners. Alternatively you could ask other boardsailors what regulations have to be complied with in that particular area. One tip: people walking and watching frequently know very little about a particular water sport area and its peculiarities, unless, of course, they are themselves boardsailors or actively involved in some type of water sport.

Ignoring local regulations can lead to a heavy fine!

While you are making enquiries, be sure to ask the very important questions which will affect your personal safety, and you will then be able to sail without danger. Does water flow

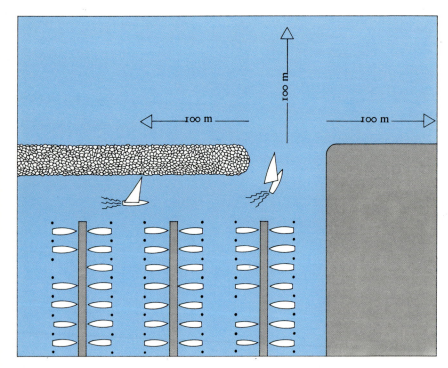

Keep at least 100 m (100 yds) away from boats' moorings and harbour entrances.

in or out of an inland reservoir or lake? At the coast, what is the effect of the ebb and flood tidal streams? Does the wind direction change regularly in the area as wind strengths differ? Is the water shallow anywhere? Are there sand banks, submerged rocks and so on?

Lack of knowledge or disregard of such local peculiarities is not an offence that leads to punishment by fine but, what is far more important, it could cause you to jeopardise your safety (and risk injury), as well as possibly damaging or losing your board. In order to keep out of danger when boardsailing, you must take into account the local characteristics and peculiarities of whatever waters you are sailing in.

What are the most suitable waters to learn on and to practise on as a beginner?

You can boardsail on small patches of water that are barely a couple of hundred metres across, because sailboards are not only among the smallest of craft but are also some of the most manoeuvrable. Although the coast may be several hours' drive away, the smallest inland waters, such as disused gravel pits, provide what a boardsailor needs.

Small inland waters are best for you as a beginner because you can easily be supervised. Even if you get blown away during your first lesson and are unable to return to your departure point, there is always a shore nearby from which you can return to your starting point on foot.

Sometimes water sports areas are

This part of the shore is unsuitable for your first attempts; it is too busy.

You can boardsail even on very small stretches of water.

used so intensively by sailors, boardsailors, children with inflatable mattresses and swimmers that there is barely enough space for your first attempts and your inevitable falls into the water. On large inland lakes or at the coast, it is generally really crowded only right at the shore.

As a beginner, however, you should stay as close to the bank as possible, and within shouting distance. You will almost always be able to find a quieter spot, probably a short distance from the direct approach from the car park, and that is where to start practising.

Best of all is if the water near the shore is shallow enough for you to stand in, because you can then push or pull your board back to the shore if you find you cannot sail it back. The water should be at least hip deep (see Climbing on to the Board, p. 54). Sometimes areas like this are specifically allocated for boardsailors.

A sandy beach or a shore with no

tion between the two. You often find that, although the wind is tousling your hair, there is a completely smooth patch of water near the shore.

This is typical of what happens when the wind direction is such that you would be running a risk if you set out on the water, because the wind must be blowing from the land towards the water. There are two reasons a land breeze or offshore wind can be dangerous, not only in the case of a beginner who is trying to find his feet for the first time, but for all boardsailors:

■ The strength of an offshore breeze is always underestimated. Wind is slowed by land and deflected by trees, houses and even the bank or shore. Waves form some distance from the shore, and so you cannot draw reliable conclusions about wind strength by looking at them.

■ An offshore wind blows you away from the land. Every time you fall or pause for a rest, you drift quickly ever further from the shore. And the further you are from the shore, the stronger the wind becomes and the higher the waves will be.

Smooth water near by the shore, therefore, must not be taken to indicate that conditions are so ideal that you must rush off with your largest sail, and without needing to take any safety precautions.

So, if you can feel an appreciable amount of wind when on land but can see no waves near the shore, take this as an indication not to set out,

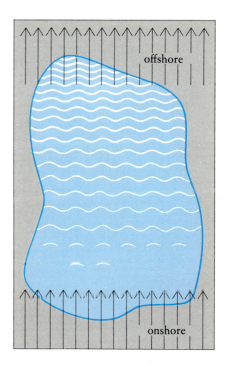

or to go only if experienced friends are near, or if there is a shore downwind of you which you can reach easily in an emergency, or if there are enough buoys in the vicinity for you to be able to tie up to one of them if the wind is strong.

When the wind is blowing towards the land, that is to say when there is a sea breeze or onshore wind, it is safe to set out, but you have to accept the fact that there are always waves near the shore when the wind blows in this direction.

If you ask boardsailors what the *ideal* wind direction is, they will all tell you that least can go wrong when the wind is blowing parallel to the shore. If you take all this into account when selecting the area to practise in, you will neither endanger yourself nor get other people into difficulties as a result of coming to

rocks is another advantage. The place where you practise should be sheltered from larger waves, because waves are particularly unwelcome when you are having difficulties anyway keeping your balance as you make your first attempts. You will feel steadier in a protected bay.

Waves are generally raised by wind, and you need to know the connec-

help you in an emergency. By the seaside, these facts may sometimes mean that you have had a wasted journey to the coast because you must *not* set out to sea when an offshore wind is blowing. On inland waters it is only a question of finding an alternative place to start from, because somewhere round the shore of a lake the wind must be onshore, or ideal as described. It does not take long to find such a place, and you should search for it, especially if you are still feeling rather unsteady on your board.

When sailing on the coast, do not go out for the first time unless you have made sure that there is a rescue service operating from your stretch of beach. Do not boardsail if the water is falling – that is, the tide is going out!

Naturally you will not always find optimum conditions, but on your first attempts you will find it much easier if you search for a place where conditions are as nearly ideal as possible.

Ideal conditions for beginners are:
Sandy or gravelly shore
Hip deep water near the shore
Protected from waves (bay)
Water temperature over 18°C (64°F)
Warm sunny weather
Light winds parallel to the shore and onshore

Nature and the environment

Today, the non-stop increase in industrialisation, the exhaust fumes of motor cars and fumes from central heating systems, indeed civilisation in general, put a heavy burden on nature and the environment in which we live. The self-cleansing, self-preservation and survival processes of nature are disturbed and plants and even whole forests die, while waters become polluted and many species of fish and birds degenerate before finally becoming extinct. Naturalists and conservationists have long recognised these problems, and laws prescribe limits for pollution of air and water by harmful products.

Fines are imposed for excesses, but it is extremely difficult to check that limits are observed. Often there is a lack of awareness of the fact that there is a responsibility to plough back commercial profit to benefit the environment and protect nature.

This depressing situation is often aggravated by the ignorance and thoughtlessness of individuals. Boardsailors need to remember that they are endangering nature even when they sail their shallow boards right up to a shore which hitherto has provided undisturbed spawning grounds for fish, or nesting and rest-

Opposite *Ideal conditions for beginners.*
Below *Too many parts of the shore look like this.*

15

ing places for many varieties of birds. Animals are disturbed while feeding, and they withdraw from their traditional habitats. Because of the early start to the boardsailing season, and the use of strong autumn winds right up to the onset of winter, some waters are used for the sport at times of year when, until now, wildlife has had exclusive use of them for breeding and resting.

The other side of the coin is that those who use waters for sporting purposes, and swimmers and boardsailors in particular, have to suffer from the severe pollution of the environment.

You can contribute to keeping waters open by your awareness of these problems and by your own conduct. A friendly warning about a conservation area, or 'forgotten' rubbish can often forestall a thoughtless or careless action.

At present, there is adequate water for us to pursue our sport. As to the future, the extent to which boardsailing and other water sports can be practised will depend on how sportsmen react to education and instruction about their behaviour in relation to the environment.

Rules for protecting the environment

1. No swimming also means no boardsailing.

2. Inquire about the quality of the water, and possible dangerous areas.

3. Look at the surface of the water, and avoid polluted areas.

4. Encourage others to care for the environment by your own example.

5. Support those who campaign for a clean environment. Remember, you need clean water for your sport.

Rules for nature conservation

◀ 1. Do not sail into reeds, or into shallows where water plants grow.

2. Keep at least 100 m (over 100 yds) ▶ away from flocks or groups of birds.

◀ 3. Observe restrictions relating to water sports in nature reserves.

4. Be considerate of all creatures ▶ near such reserves.

◀ 5. Use only official landing places and areas where you cannot harm animals.

6. Keep at least 30–50 m (or yds) ▶ away from dense vegetation by the water's edge, on land as well.

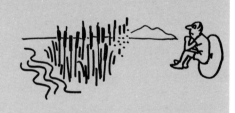

◀ 7. Keep at least 300–500 m (or yds) away from areas where seals bask, and from bird islands.

8. Observe and photograph ▶ animals only from a distance.

◀ 9. Keep the water clean.

10. Find out what regulations ▶ are in force in your area.

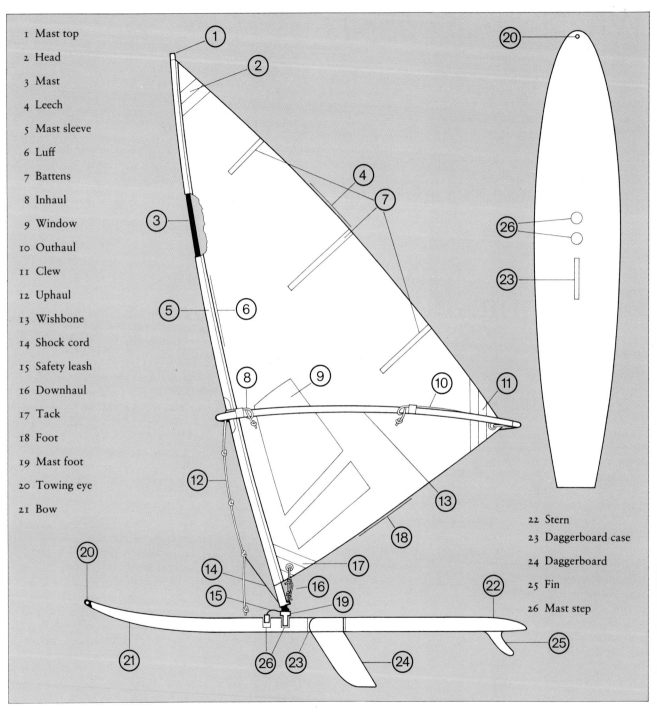

What is a sailboard?

Take a look at the diagram opposite which shows all the important parts of a complete sailboard. There is a specific term for every part, and you should note them because you will need to know what the parts are called when you are learning how to boardsail. You will soon find that the terms relating to your equipment become second nature.

A sailboard has two major parts – the board and the rig. The vital parts of the board are the fin, the daggerboard and the holes: the slot for the daggerboard (the daggerboard case), the hole for the mast (the mast step), and the towing eye at the bow.

The rig is more complicated. Rig is the term used for the sailboard's 'motor' which consists of mast, mast foot, wishbone boom, sail, and the lines needed to connect the parts to each other.

Basic equipment for a beginner

If you want to buy your own sailboard, you have some important decisions to make initially. How much money do I want to spend on this sport? Shall I buy a new board, or will a second-hand one do to begin with? What additional equipment is necessary or advisable?

The sailboard market offers such an enormous variety now that even experts can barely keep track, and it is therefore only possible to give a summary of current rigs, types of boards and the various materials from which a board is made. The decision as to which make to buy depends mainly on how well you can sail, on your standards, on how much you want to spend, and on the area where you will sail most frequently.

So far as sailing characteristics, equipment and price are concerned, there is very little to choose between several makes and it may well be that it is the attractive designs on the board and the sail that help you to make up your mind.

Notes on the rig

The *mast* is always matched to the sail that is delivered with it. Masts differ mainly in their diameter and in how flexible they are.

First turn your attention to the *mast foot*, which is the link between board and rig. It incorporates a rubber, plastic or universal joint which enables the rig to be moved in all directions while still staying connected to the board. An important feature is that it should have a release mechanism which can be adjusted, preferably without tools. You need to be able to release the mast from the board without difficulty at certain moments, but it should be so firmly stepped in the board while you are sailing that it will not slip out of the slot when you haul the rig out of the water, or every time you fall in. You must also be able to attach a strong *leash* or safety line to the mast foot; this will provide a secure connection between the rig and the board, and prevent the board from drifting away should the mast foot release itself.

There is little difference in the outward appearance of the wishbone *booms* produced by the various manufacturers, but they do vary in stability of shape (how much they will give when under load), length (to match the sail) and cross-section of the tube, as well as in how good a grip the sheath provides. Booms are made of sea-water resistant alum-

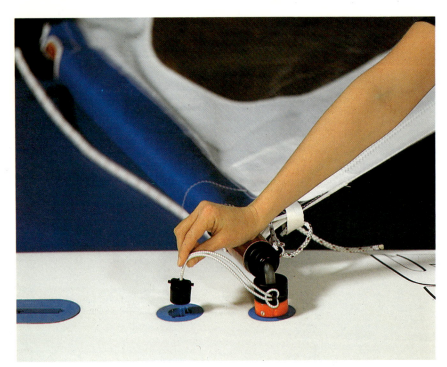

Above *Every sailboard must have a safety leash to connect the rig to the board.*
Opposite *You can test the quality of the rig best by trying it out.*

inium tubing of round, oval or octagonal section. It is best to try them yourself to see which section you find easiest to grasp. The rubber sheathing must also be easy to grip, and resistant to wear so that it will not tear and strip away from the boom the first time you catch it on a sharp stone.

It is very difficult indeed for a novice to judge the quality of a *sail*. It is often only after a considerable period that a sail proves whether it is good or bad in that, after frequent use, it either keeps its shape or becomes limp and baggy.

Signs of a good sail are: regular seams, with no stitching faults; reinforcement at the corners; a large window with no crinkles or cracks; a high enough cut-out in the mast sleeve to enable the boom to be attached to the mast at the right height; abrasion resistant sailcloth.

New sailboards are generally equipped either with a racing sail about 6 sq m (65 sq ft) in area with battens, or with a medium-sized sail of about 5.6 sq m (60 sq ft) without battens. Before buying, you should assemble the rig completely and set it up in the wind to check that the sail fills with virtually no creases (see Assembling the Rig, p. 33).

Notes on the board

The terms used for sailboards can be misleading. For example, an allround board is no less enjoyable to sail than a funboard. In any case with a funboard the fun only starts when the wind is strong, whereas an allround board shows its strengths in light to moderate winds. In general, board types are differentiated according to how they are used, and by their suitability for different wind conditions and for individuals of varying ability.

Allround board: Length about 3.6–3.9 m (11 ft 9 in–12 ft 9 in). Weight about 20 kg (44 lb). Swivelling centreboard, stable. For sailing in winds of Force 1 to 5; performs well in light breezes. A good board for learners.

Allround-Funboard: Length about 3.4–3.7 m (11–12 ft). Weight about 18 kg ($39\frac{1}{2}$ lb). Daggerboard case further aft; vario daggerboard. Better strong wind characteristics; moderately stable. For Force 1–6 winds; performs well in moderate winds. Usable, but not ideal, as a board for beginners.

Funboard: Length about 2.5–3.5 m (8 ft 3 in–11 ft 6 in). Maximum weight 17 kg ($37\frac{1}{2}$ lb). No daggerboard, or possibly a small vario; one to three fins; not stable. For sailing in winds of Force 4 and above; very good strong wind characteristics. Not suitable for beginners.

Allround board, complete with rig.

Displacement board: Length about 3.9 m (12 ft 9 in). Weight at least 18 kg (39½ lb). Large daggerboard or swivel centreboard; not very stable due to round bottom. Racing board; Force 1–4; very good light breeze characteristics. Not suitable for beginners.

There is no clear dividing line between the four types of board described above, and there are many compromise designs in various manufacturers' leaflets. As someone new to boardsailing, you should select a board which is versatile and which you will enjoy, even on your first attempts to sail. Boards with the following characteristics have proved to be suitable for this purpose:

- Tough skin (see Material, p. 24)
- No heavier than 20–22 kg (44–48½ lb)
- Adequate volume, at least 200 litres (44 gals)
- Not too narrow at the stern
- Flat-bottomed
- Large swivelling centreboard, or a vario daggerboard of adequate size (see photograph)
- Non-slip standing surface

Above *From top: Allround board, Allround-funboard, funboard, extreme funboard.*
Below *1. Vario daggerboard   2. Mini vario daggerboard   3. Fin   4. Swing-back daggerboard   5. Storm daggerboard. The board would just drift sideways if it had no daggerboard or fin. The fin also provides directional stability.*

Boards with these features come into the allround or allround-funboard categories. They are sufficiently stable and behave well.

At present, prices vary from about £250 for a cheap allround board up to £1,000 for a racing displacement board.

Material

Not only do you need information about the type of board, but also about the material of which a board is made. Almost all manufacturers provide a polyurethane foam or expanded polystyrene core. It is important to remember that if a board has a polystyrene core it may only be repaired with epoxy resin because polyester resin dissolves polystyrene.

The solid outer skin of a board is usually made of one of the following materials:

Materials	Advantages	Disadvantages
GRP, glassfibre reinforced plastics	Minor damage can be repaired by amateurs. Lightweight	Brittle, damaged by knocks
ABS/ASA thermoplastic (heat-moulded plastics)	Tough, minor damage can be repaired easily	Rather heavier, major damage has to be repaired by an expert
Polyethylene, hot blown into a mould or spun (thermoplastic)	Very tough	Relatively heavy, damage can only be repaired by an expert

Tools

Always take a small tool kit and repair kit with you:

> Screwdriver, knife (rigid blade), combination pliers; also a lighter for melting the ends of synthetic fibre ropes, and waterproof adhesive tape for making temporary patches to repair minor damage to board and sail; some glassfibre, polyester or epoxy resin, plus suitable filler and sandpaper.

Spare parts

Nothing is more infuriating than to be away on holiday somewhere, in ideal weather, and to have to abandon boardsailing, just because of some small mishap. You should always carry a few spares in the car with you, most importantly:

> - a complete set of lines
> - a second mast foot
> - spare battens
> - possibly a spare fin

Buying second-hand

Buying a second-hand board has to be largely a matter of trust, because it is virtually impossible to detect internal damage to the mast or the board. Be careful if you are buying a board that has been used hard for more than one season, and be sure to check the following points:

Board checklist
- Weight of the board. If it is much heavier than the manufacturer's advertised weight, it will have absorbed water and be unusable.
- Does it have any soft spots? Does the outer skin adhere to the core everywhere? Check this by pressing with the flat of your hand.
- Are the sides undamaged?
- Do the mast foot, daggerboard and fin fit in their slots properly?
- Is daggerboard or fin damaged?
- Has the board got a towing eye and is there a safety leash for the rig?

Rig checklist
- If repairs have been necessary, have they been carried out skilfully? (The mast should show no signs whatsoever of having been damaged.)
- The boom should not be bent.
- Is the rubber sheathing round the boom free of damage, and are the cleats and the parts which connect the tubing firmly fixed?
- Is the wishbone boom watertight (no water inside it)?
- Is the sail undamaged (no tears, holes, worn seams, torn batten pockets or mildew?)
- Is the mast foot in order, and does the adjustment mechanism function properly?

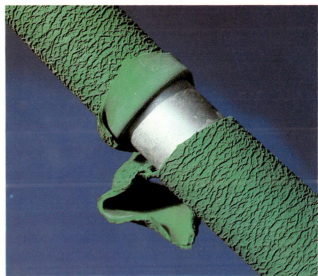

Above left *Damage to the mast is normally discovered only when the mast breaks.*
Above right *The sheathing round the boom is damaged.*
Below left *Typical sail damage: a burst seam.*
Below right *Torn sail.*

Sometimes it pays to buy a new sail for a second-hand rig, because the sail always suffers from wear and tear, and in any case has only a limited life. Even if you buy a brand-new sailboard, you will have to purchase a new sail eventually.

It is difficult to decide whether to buy a new or a second-hand board. The advantage of buying new is that you have the benefit of the manufacturer's guarantee, but you can equally enjoy years of fun with a good second-hand board.

After you have bought the essentials, check what extras you will need for yourself and your family.

Additional equipment

It is sensible to buy a smaller sail and what is called a storm daggerboard so that you are still able to control the board when the wind blows harder. There are also some vario wishbone booms which can be adjusted in length; they can then be used shortened with the smaller sail or lengthened with the larger. If you have no objections to advertising, you could buy a small sail quite cheaply, because a number of manufacturers offer really good quality sails of all sizes with advertisements on them.

Your children may also be interested in boardsailing and want to learn too. This is great, because it is much more fun when the whole family sets off excitedly to sail together. A smaller sail will then be absolutely essential. Although children can start to learn at about ten years old and upwards, and will soon be able to control 'their' board at that age, most of them are not strong enough to haul the large sail out of the water. It might be sensible to buy a complete child's or junior rig, which consists of a small sail, a shorter and thinner boom, and a shorter and very light mast, but, of course, a child's rig is pretty expensive.

The pleasure that your family takes in boardsailing will have its disadvantages, because more and more often you will only see your sailboard from a distance. Don't be upset – watching is fun too!

Clothing

In our latitudes you can virtually count on two hands the days when you can boardsail in swimming gear in the heat of high summer.

Water and wind are part and parcel of boardsailing. The coldness which results when water or wet skin evaporates is very noticeable, and you will start to feel freezing cold much sooner than the 'sun worshippers' who are lying on the shore in a spot sheltered from the wind. You cannot, therefore, do without clothing that will keep you warm and at the same time protect you from injury and sunburn.

Unless you know your way around, you will certainly be confused by the variety of clothing that is on offer, and the following points will help you to choose.

Most boardsailing clothing is made of neoprene, an extremely elastic black foam material with fine pores.

No water can force its way into a dry suit.

When you fall in, the suit absorbs some water. The material lying close to the skin, and the thin film of water on your skin, warm up to body temperature and so provide good insulation against colder seawater. Boardsailing clothing must fit well without creases, so that no extra water can flow in to take the place of water that has already been heated to body temperature. If water is exchanged in this way your body temperature is lowered rapidly, and you will soon be extremely cold despite wearing your wetsuit.

The neoprene used for boardsailing purposes is 3–4 mm ($\frac{1}{8}$ in) thick. Diver's suits are made of thicker material, but they are not so suitable for boardsailing because they are cut differently, and allow less movement for your shoulders and arms.

The exterior of boardsailing clothing is either smooth and shiny (black) or is covered with coloured material. There are pros and cons to both. *Uncovered* neoprene wetsuits absorb no water on the exterior, which means less loss of heat due to

Left *Long johns.*
Centre *Complete wetsuit.*
Right *Buoyancy aids provide extra buoyancy.*

evaporation. However neoprene is soft and therefore very susceptible to damage. Black neoprene also becomes very hot in the sun – which is an advantage in cold temperatures, of course. One tip: the knees of plain neoprene clothing should be reinforced with material because that is where wear is greatest.

With *covered* wetsuits, there is a greater choice of modern designs. Because of the covering they are less likely to be damaged, but they are not so warm because of the water absorbed in the outer layer of material. Furthermore, they do not stretch as easily as uncovered suits. There are 6 mm ($\frac{1}{4}$ in) neoprene suits for boardsailors whose season extends beyond the summer, and also what are called *drysuits*. These are made of thin synthetic fibre material, and do not themselves provide heat, but they are totally watertight at the neck, wrist and ankle openings and water really is kept out. You have to wear suitable clothing, thermal underwear or a tracksuit, underneath.

In our climate, it is best to have a two-part suit with long johns (trousers with sleeveless top) and a long-sleeved jacket. You can then wear either the long johns alone or the complete suit, depending on the weather.

For summer sailing there are lightweight wetsuits with long or short legs, made of thin synthetic material, and there are wetsuits with short legs (shorties), but clothing of this sort is only suitable for very warm days.

Shoes are an absolute must if you are to avoid injuring your feet by getting them caught between the mast foot and the board, or when stepping on sharp stones or slivers of glass on shore. An ordinary pair of training shoes with non-slip soles will do. You may want neoprene boardsailing shoes, or at least neoprene socks to keep your feet warm.

Should you become a 'tough' boardsailor who is not put off by the cold storms of autumn, you will also need a neoprene hood and gloves.

You must also buy a comfortable buoyancy aid which will help you to float when you fall into the water; on some inland waters such as reservoirs, regulations state that personal buoyancy must be worn, and it is also essential when you are sailing on larger lakes or at the coast. A small tip: take a plastic bucket or a large plastic bag with you – wet neoprene clothing holds a surprisingly large amount of water.

The journey to your sailing area

Very few boardsailors indeed are able to sail on water which is right next to their house, but everybody must have dreamed of one day being able to take a ready-rigged sailboard directly from the garage to the water, and then to be able to park it back there again when a long day of boardsailing has ended or when strength and wind have failed.

A few people do at least succeed in getting close to this idyllic state when they are on holiday and can hire a board from a sailing school, or leave their own board there, but otherwise there is always the same ceremony to be performed as a preliminary to a sail. Preparation gradually becomes mere routine and takes up very little time, but it is easy to become careless about minor matters and this can sometimes spoil a whole day and your good humour.

One advantage that the boardsailor has over a small boat sailor is that it takes much less time to pack up and transport a board and its gear, this is one of the reasons why the sport is so popular. If you make a routine of the following rules and suggestions for packing up and transporting your board and gear, all will be ready and secure in the minimum of time, and you will have gained extra time to spend sailing out on the water. If you waste no time, it makes a free hour on the water at the end of a working day worth while.

Permitted load

Did you know that there is a limit to how much you are allowed to carry on your car roof? You may find a note in the car handbook telling you how much the manufacturer states is permissible, or you may have to search for it in the workshop manual or perhaps even ask the manufacturer.

The permitted load for your car will be somewhere between 25 kg and 100 kg (55–220 lb). If you have a smaller car, it is important to check the figure allowed; with a larger car you can assume that you may load at least one sailboard on the roof. If you calculate the weight of the individual parts and add that to the weight of the board you will find that the mast and wishbone boom together increase the weight of the board on the scales by as much as 6 kg (13 lb). Two complete sailboards therefore can weigh as much as 100kg (220 lb).

> Regardless of how many boards you load on your car roof, the total weight or maximum load must not 'be such as to be likely to cause danger to anyone on the road or in the car'. The distribution of a load can be held to be dangerous.

Roof rack

The difference between normal baggage roof racks and those designed for sailboards is that the latter are particularly wide and have strong attachment catches, because a sailboard roof rack not only has to cope with considerable weight but also has to stand up to the enormous wind forces which result from fast driving. A roof rack for a single sailboard should be certified as capable of carrying at least 50 kg (110 lb), and the actual figure should be shown in the manufacturer's leaflet. Even though you will normally only want to take one board to the water, bear in mind that you may sometimes need to take a second with you for some reason, if you are going to a surf beach, for example, or when accompanied by a friend.

Another point is that the roof rack must be quick and easy to attach. If you leave it on the roof when just going out for a drive, you will spend a good deal more on extra petrol. The easier that a roof rack can be fitted and removed, the more readily will you take it off after use. You learn from experience that if you need to use a special tool to remove a roof rack, or if it takes a long time to put it on and take it off, it will spend the whole summer stuck on the roof quite unnecessarily. Furthermore, a long term session on the roof like this means that you do not regularly check the catches which hold it, and, if you have to brake hard, the whole of your valuable load, together with the roof rack, could well slip forward and off the roof – the consequence in a busy street can be imagined only too easily!

Not every make of roof rack fits every car roof. For example, if it is impossible to attach the roof rack to the rainwater gutter, or if the curve of the roof is excessive, or if you drive a convertible, you will have to go to a specialist or ask the car manufacturer's advice. Special racks have now been made for virtually every make of car.

Right The locks must be done up when you leave the car.
Below The components of an anti-theft sailboard roof rack.

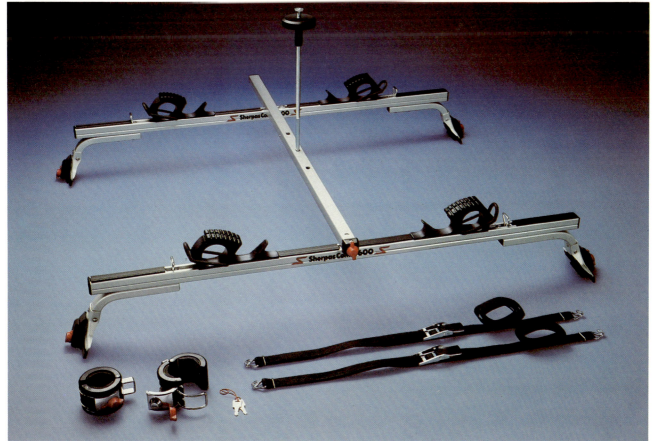

Anti-theft measures

Unfortunately, some people who have become interested in boardsailing do not buy their boards but pinch them. If you want to stop your board from being stolen, if, for example, it has to be left for some time unsupervised with all your gear on the roof, you would be wise to invest a few extra pounds and buy a roof rack that deters thieves. Sailboard insurance alone will not protect you from the consequences of theft. Insurance policies state (usually only in small print) exactly what preventative measures you yourself must take against theft. Some policies even stipulate that certain makes of roof rack must be used. Sailboard third party, fire and theft insurances, with or without excess in the case of damage, include other rules concerning damage, and you can be certain that the insurer will not accept liability for damage which you, unintentionally of course, inflict on other people. In a collision with another vessel on the water, for example, only a suitable personal liability policy will cover you.

When loading the board on to the roof rack, take particular care that the mast and wishbone boom, as well as the board, can be locked up and see that the locks are secure when the car is left.

Loading up the roof rack

The principle is to place the board on the roof rack bow forward and

Roof rack, board and mast must not protrude forwards or sideways.

Car-top transport and the law

■ The law says that a load carried by a car or trailer must never be such as to cause danger, or be likely to cause danger, to anyone on the road or in the car. A court would probably hold that an offence had been committed if a sailboard or its equipment stuck out sideways or far beyond the back of the vehicle.

Hints on carrying a sailboard on the roof:

■ Do not exceed the permitted roof load! Driving characteristics are affected, especially on corners and in side winds.
■ Check the permitted roof rack load with the manufacturers.
■ After use, take off the roof rack (fuel consumption, theft, rust etc).
■ Fit anti-theft device.
■ Place the board correctly, and avoid causing pressure dents.
■ Only pull the straps as tight as will prevent the board from shifting on the roof rack – ie, no more than necessary.
■ Check frequently that the roof rack straps, shock cord and load are secure when making a long journey.

bottom up. Aerodynamically this is the most satisfactory way when motoring at higher speeds; you can drive up to 130 km/h (80 mph) quite safely. The roof rack should be cushioned with suitable foam or rubber padding. Only strong synthetic fibre webbing straps should be used to secure the board, with the straps pulled just tight enough to prevent the board from moving. Don't just use brute force when tightening the straps; be sensitive. For example, 'as tight as possible' is wrong because pulling the straps too hard can cause ugly depressions in some materials. The board will then be dented even before you have used it for the first time, and its sailing characteristics will certainly be affected if the bottom is uneven.

Even more important is to check that the tension of the straps is right after you have motored a short distance, especially if it has rained, and if you have a long drive, check them at every stop because the position of the board alters and straps can stretch. The boom may be attached above or below the board, depending on the make of roof rack. On lockable racks, it is generally clamped beneath the board. If the boom is placed on top of the board, check that the sheathing round the boom is not damaged by the straps. To protect the boom sheathing, you can strap the board on first, and then attach the boom above or beside it with shock cord.

The mast should be effectively clamped into the appropriate fittings. It is advisable to have these mast holders even if they have to be bought separately because, although it can be done, it is tedious fastening the mast securely with ropes or shock cord. Anti-theft devices are available for masts as well. When loading gear, check that neither board nor mast protrude forward or sideways beyond the car. Nor should the roof rack itself be wider than the car; if it is, it must be shortened with a saw. An overhang of up to about 1 m (3 ft) at the back does not matter, but if the overlap is greater a warning such as a red cloth by day or a red light by night, should be attached to the overhanging part where it can be seen.

Before going abroad, check on the regulations relating to car-top transport; these vary from country to country, for instance, overhang is sometimes specified and specific signs have to be given.

Driving with a board on the roof

The extra weight on the roof will affect your car's performance; you will notice this particularly on the bends. You should, in any case, gradually accustom yourself to driving with a heavy weight on the roof. The extra weight and the increased resistance of a board on top of the car particularly affect acceleration when overtaking, and the amount of petrol consumed. You will also notice side winds much more than when you are motoring with nothing on the roof.

Have you remembered everything?

Before you leave home, take the time to check whether you have forgotten anything. You wouldn't believe how often you can leave something behind.

You are most likely to forget the battens. You can use the sail without them, of course, but it will not set or draw properly. It really is most annoying if you leave the daggerboard, fin, mast foot or ropes at home. You often hear questions like 'Can you lend me a line – I've left my inhaul behind'.

Even when you are in a rush because the wind and weather are just right and you have only a short time to spare, run quickly through the following checklist before you set off.

On the roof:
board, wishbone boom, mast
In the back:
sailbag
sail (large/small)
3 battens (spare?)
mast foot
daggerboard (normal/storm daggerboard)
3 ropes (inhaul, outhaul, downhaul)
spare rope (minimum 3 m (10 ft) long)
Clothing and other items:
wet- or drysuit
boardsailing shoes
towel
tools
repair kit
spares

In spite of being hungry, tired and in a hurry, use the same checklist when you are preparing to return home. Beaches are not the best places to return the next day to try and find something left behind.

From the car park to the water

You rarely find a car park right by the shore, and often you have to take your board and gear quite some distance to the water. This is much easier if you have one of the transporters which can be bought from specialist shops. These vary from simple straps with which to carry the board, to convenient wheeled carriages.

If you are without such an aid, the easiest way of carrying the board is to slip one hand round it and into the daggerboard case, then grip the mast foot with the other (see p. 47).

Right Very practical: rollers fitted to the fin slots.
Below Collapsible surf-caddy.

32

Assembling the rig

Before starting to rig the board, that is, to put the parts together, it is best to sort out the various components, especially if yours is a new rig. That way everything will be packed separately.

All these separate parts make up a complete sailboard.

Parts of the rig
- Sail with the battens that belong to it
- Mast foot with safety leash
- Uphaul (a thick rope with which the rig is raised from the water)
- Outhaul (a long line which tensions the sail inside the wishbone boom)
- Inhaul (which holds the boom to the mast)
- Downhaul (which connects the lowest point of the sail, the tack, to the mast foot)

Some sailboards are still delivered with no assembly instructions, but you can read below how to rig them correctly. You must also learn how to tie a few special knots.

Knots

Knots used by seamen hold securely, and can be released easily when necessary. Many landlubber's knots will hold too, but often they can only be undone by cutting the rope. You should practise tying the proper knots until you can do them in your sleep, because you will need to use them every time you go boardsailing to ensure that your rig is assembled really securely and will not come to pieces the first time you fall in.

Figure of eight knot: prevents a line from slipping right through a cleat. Tie one at the end of every line.

Reef knot: used to connect two ropes of the same size.

Half hitch: a safeguard; tied to prevent a line from releasing itself from a cleat.

Timber hitch: the usual mast to boom connection, but when pulled tight, it can be difficult to release.

Mast loop: simplest method of attaching the boom to the mast without the boom being able to slip.

Bowline: knot with which a non-slip loop is made; to be used when being towed, or to attach the downhaul to the tack.

Try tying and untying these knots again and again with your eyes shut; take every opportunity to practise!

Above left *Figure of eight knot.*
Below left *Reef knot.*
Right *Half hitch with a figure of eight knot by the outhaul cleat.*

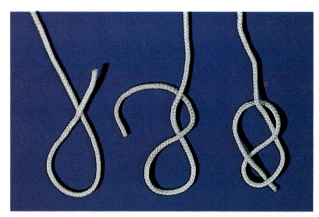

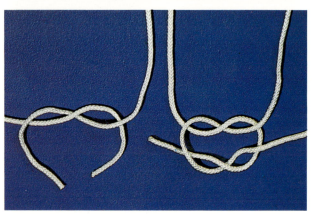

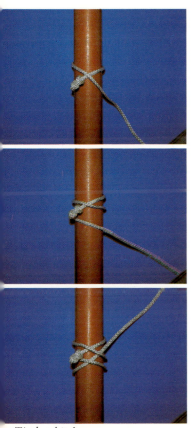

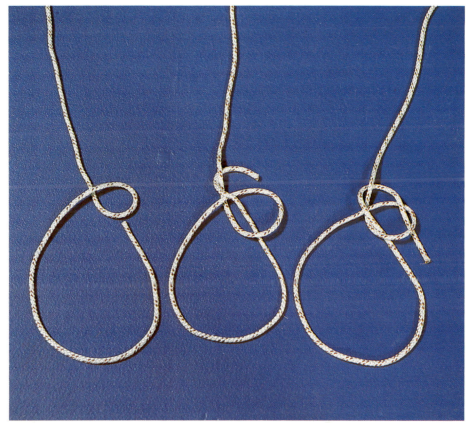

Timber hitch. *Bowline.*

Make a loop round the mast. *Mast loop slack.* *Mast loop pulled tight.*

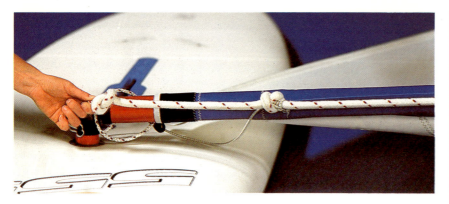

Above *The uphaul must reach right to the mast foot.*

1 Spread out the sail; slip the mast into the mast sleeve.

Rigging

Now we can start to rig the board. The first step (in the case of a new board only) is to attach the uphaul to the boom. Hold the boom with the cleats on top and lead the uphaul from beneath through the large hole at the forward end of the boom. Prevent it from slipping out again by tying a simple overhand knot or a figure of eight knot. Now tie three or four overhand knots in the uphaul, equal distances apart, with the last at the bottom end. The uphaul should be long enough to reach to the foot of the mast when the rig has been assembled. Use three or four half hitches to attach the shock cord to the uphaul about 40 cm (15 in) above the lowest knot, so that it extends some way below the lowest knot. The uphaul and shock cord will now stay permanently attached to the boom. You will often find that the uphaul supplied with a mass-produced board is too short when the boom is set at the right height. The uphaul should extend right down to the mast foot; if it does not, you have to undo all bar the lowest knot, and then fit a longer uphaul as soon as possible. The next steps are simpler, and it is best to proceed in the following order.

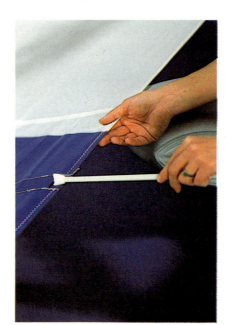

5 The wedges on the sail battens go in first.

6 Stand the mast upright, and attach the inhaul to the mast at eye level.

2 Fit the mast foot into the mast. Attach the downhaul to the eye in the tack with a bowline.

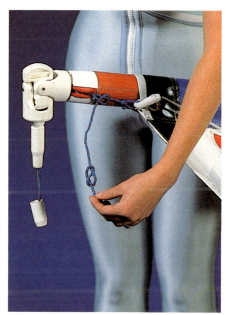

3 Tension the luff of the sail with the downhaul, and secure with a half hitch and figure of eight.

4 Place the battens in the batten pockets.

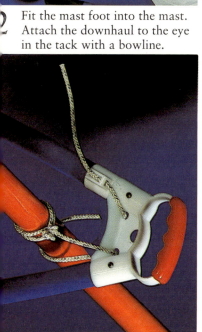

7 Attach the wishbone boom to the mast . . .

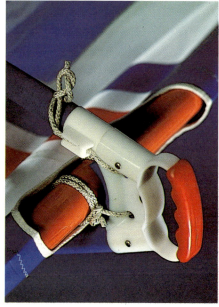

8 . . . securing the inhaul with a half hitch and a figure of eight knot.

9 Hook the shock cord to the downhaul.

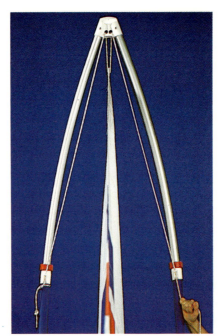
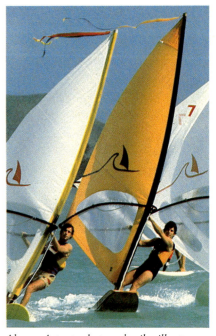

10 Extend the sail by pulling on the outhaul until there are no creases in it when it is full of wind.

11 The outhaul should look like a large M; secure the free end of the outhaul with a half hitch and a figure of eight knot.

Above *A properly tuned sail will set without creases.*
Below left *Rig left lying on the beach. It will be unusable after a night pounded by surf.*
Opposite right *Drying sails in a sail rack: not advisable when the wind is strong.*

Some sailboards have a mechanical connection between the mast and wishbone boom, and they need no inhaul. The boom is then simply latched into a fitting on the mast. The hinging mechanism of the daggerboard also varies from maunufacturer to manufacturer, so you need to check on these details carefully in the shop.

Tuning the sail

The individual cloths which are seamed together to make up a sail are cut in such a way as to give the sail a curved profile, called camber. The position of the deepest point and the depth of camber are affected by the way you tune the sail, though if yours is a good sail and well matched to the mast and boom that you are using, you have little scope for adjustment because the cut of the sail prescribes a camber which tuning can only slightly alter. Tuning a sail correctly is largely a question of experience, and requires great sensitivity.

Horizontal creases in a sail indicate that the downhaul is not sufficiently taut; vertical creases parallel to the mast show that outhaul tension should be increased. Downhaul and outhaul tension must be matched to each other. If creases reappear when your sail is wet, you have to retune it carefully. A sail with a nylon mast sleeve can only be tuned after it has become wet because wet nylon stretches a great deal.

Care of your equipment

Now that you know how to prepare your board for sailing, it is time to think for a moment about how to look after your equipment so that it will last as long as possible. The sail is the part of your sailboard which is most susceptible to damage and which wears out fastest.

A few suggestions on sail care:
- Never let your rig lie on the shore half in and half out of the water. Even the smallest waves will make the rig move and a hole will soon be rubbed in the sail.
- When taking a rest on shore, always ease the outhaul, and perhaps the downhaul as well, so as to avoid stretching the sail unnecessarily and making it baggy. The sail will not fill with wind once the tension has been released.
- After sailing in salt water, rinse the sail in fresh water.
- Before folding up the sail, dry it thoroughly, preferably without laying it out in the blazing sun. Special rig racks are set up in some areas for this purpose.

■ If you have to pack your sail away wet, wrap it round the mast and then hang it out to dry at home.
■ The following method is best when folding and stowing a sail: start at the foot and fold it back and forth like an S; keep straight up the line of the leech, which will mean that the mast sleeve zigzags. Be careful to avoid damaging the window by bending it. Roll up the sail, leech first, and put it in the sail bag.

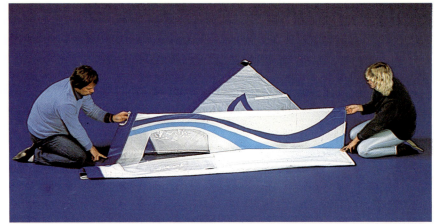

Take good care of your board too:
■ Stand on the board only when daggerboard and fin are clear of the bottom.
■ Do not sail right up on to the beach – just because it looks 'cool'. This is hard on the board, daggerboard and fin.
■ Do not lay your board on the beach bottom down; the fin can break off.
■ Blazing sunshine is not good for boards. Some plastic boards may blister.
■ Do not put your board in the water if it has even a small hole. The core will absorb water, and you will not be able get rid of it later.

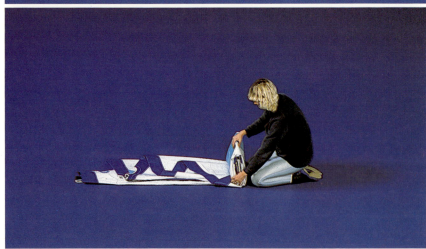

Checking on board and rig

How very pleasant and convenient it is to borrow a sailboard from a friend, or hire one from a boardsailing school. Thinking happily that you have saved the time it takes to rig the board, you sail off straight away. But such a trusting attitude can land you in trouble.
■ Are you sure that the person using the board before you has assembled the rig efficiently, and that nothing is damaged?
■ Is the wishbone boom at the right height for you?

Never neglect to check over an assembled board on which you propose to put to sea. Take the time to put right whatever may be wrong while you are still on shore. You will sometimes find that you have to unrig completely in order to re-assemble it correctly. Never use a rig that has been put together sloppily, because a fault in the equipment could get you into difficulties when you are far from the shore.

Left *How to fold up a sail correctly.*
Below *Always keep a spare line at the end of the wishbone boom.*
Right *The places to check when your sailboard has already been rigged.*

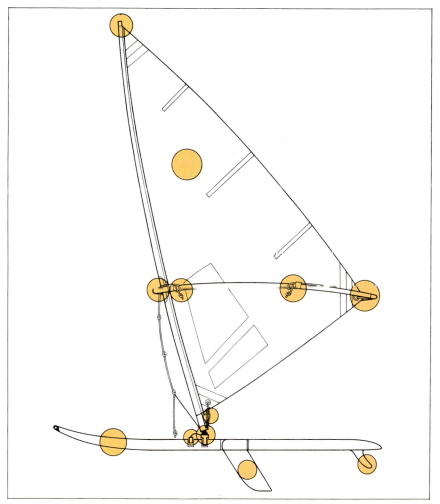

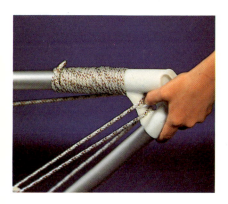

The following items should be checked if you are to sail a rigged sailboard:
■ Is the sail OK (no holes, tears, or gaping seams)?
■ Are the screws that hold the boom together screwed tight, and is the boom attached to the mast at eye level?
■ Are the lines all in working order?
■ Is the sail tuned correctly?
■ Have the right knots been tied in the right places?
■ Is the mast foot working properly?
■ Has the board got a safety leash?
■ Are the board, fin and daggerboard undamaged?
■ Is there a spare line for you to take?

41

Unrigging on the water — practised on land

1 Release the safety leash and pull out the mast foot.

2 Unhook the shock cord from the downhaul.

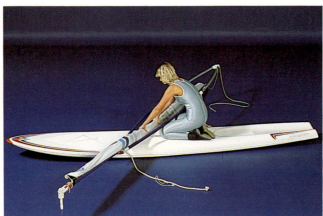

5 Fold the boom up to the mast (if you have a special mast-to-boom linkage, this has to be disconnected first).

6 Use the uphaul and shock cord to lash the sail to the mast, working towards the top of the mast.

Once the sailboard has been assembled properly, you can set out on the water with no misgivings, but what will you do if the wind drops away, or if you find, after trying for some time, that you cannot return to the place you started from? With a bit of luck you may find someone who will tow you home. If not, you will have to paddle, and that is no disgrace. Whether you are towed home or paddle yourself back, you first have to pack up the rig carefully and correctly.

It is, therefore, well worth taking the time to practise unrigging your board in peace and quiet on land. To do this, lay the board in the sand with the sail tensioned correctly and the mast foot in the mast step. It is best to kneel on the board, as you would do in practice.

If you follow the instructions given below, nothing untoward should occur out on the water. Once you have packed up the rig, you can paddle either lying down or kneeling. Having tried this out on land, you will have no difficulty on the water if a real emergency arises.

3 Pull the end of the boom towards you, and release one end of the outhaul.

4 Roll the sail up from the foot to the mast; you can leave the battens in the sail.

7 Use the free end of the outhaul to lash the sail to the mast, working towards the foot.

8 Place the parcelled-up rig on the board; the mast foot can either stick out forward of the bow, or be fitted into the mast step.

Playing and practising with board and rig

When you climb on to your board for the first time, you will realise immediately just how wobbly it is. In the main, good balance is something that you are born with, although it can be improved to some extent with practice. Often it is only one's anxiety not to fall in that causes unsteadiness on the sailboard. Even proficient swimmers suffer from a psychological fear of being totally submerged, of finding themselves beneath the sail, or of getting entangled with weed. But your anxiety will soon diminish, and you will then forget about feeling so terribly unsteady on your sailboard.

It is sensible to start with some preliminary exercises on and in the water, although they are not absolutely necessary. When you learn in a group, practising like this is great fun and you not only learn how to stay on the board but also how to fall 'correctly' into the water. But first an important tip: when beside or on the water you have to protect yourself from sunburn. But the anti-sunburn creams and oils you use will gradually build up a greasy layer on your board, making the roughened standing surface useless, and you will slip about on it helplessly. The only answer is to scrub your board down with soap and water.

Practising with the board

■ Move from the stern to the bow without falling in, in spite of first the bow and then the stern rising high out of the water.
■ Stand level with the daggerboard case, place your feet on the sides of the board to right and left of the slot, and weight your legs alternately.
■ Crouch down several times in quick succession.
■ Jump and land surely (be careful to land on both feet simultaneously).
■ Do a headstand on the board.
■ Stand on the board with a friend, one at the bow, one at the stern. Change places!
■ Practise jumping off the board, feet first *never* head first. Bend your legs slightly.
■ Dive under the board both from side to side and lengthwise.

Practising with board and rig

■ Dive under the sail.
■ Swim under the sail, raising it to let in air.
■ Turn the board over so that the daggerboard points upwards; then turn it right way up again.

> Important: Make sure that you only practise in water that is deep enough (at least hip deep). You will then avoid injuring yourself!

Games and safety rules for children

When you are practising improving your balance in this way, you will discover what fun it can be to play about with the board on occasions when there is no wind. You will understand your youngsters when they shout to you from the shore, 'I want to play with the big board now!' The sailboard really is an ideal plaything for the whole family, not just for children. It is unsinkable, and can be moved fast with very little effort by a child; air mattresses and inflatable boats are much more dangerous. You could perhaps give your child a paddle so that he can propel it effortlessly.

The sailboard is fun to play with, and not just for children.

You must observe a few safety rules at all times to prevent play from becoming dangerous. Children should:
- wear a buoyancy aid whenever the water is too deep for them to stand – even if they are able to swim,
- be shown how to paddle the board,
- always stay near the shore,
- never take the board out on to the water when the wind is blowing offshore – the danger of their drifting away from land is too great,
- never take the board out when waves are high or in surf; the board can be spun round very forcefully by the waves, or even flung into the air.

Remember that children who are playing and tumbling about do not notice when they become blue with cold. Fetch them out of the water in good time.

Children who are still too small to sail are not the only ones who find a sailboard is a splendid plaything; everyone who loves water does! As to how you can use it, well, some examples of popular games are:
- First to the buoy and back.
- Fox-hunt – many children chasing after a single 'fox'.
- Slalom through a line of buoys.
- Who can do a headstand on the board?
- How many children can get on to one board?
- Ball games in the water, using the board.

Taking the board and rig to the water

You can only put your board and rig into the water if there is enough space right by the shore. The rig, in particular, is somewhat unwieldy, and can run away with you if it is carried wrongly. The job is easy provided that you start correctly. First take your board straight to the water's edge, but do not put it into the water yet because, depending on the wind direction, it could drift away quickly. When the rig is laid in the water it will hardly drift at all, and that is why you always put the rig in first.

It is best to lift the extended rig up by the mast foot, and to turn it so that the wind gets beneath it. If there is enough wind, it will lift the sail which will line itself up with the wind. Maintain this position with the mast foot pointing towards the wind as you carry the rig, with one hand grasping the mast above the wishbone boom, and the other the boom itself, near its centre. Now lift the rig above your head and carry it to the water. Watch out for the wind direction: if the mast foot does not point towards the wind, you may no longer be able to hold the sail. Provided that the wind is strong enough, it will get beneath the rig and help you to carry it.

If you still find it difficult, try again and again in very varying conditions; however, it is best not to experiment when the shore is crowded. Just bundle up your sail, bend the boom up to the mast, and lash it there with the outhaul, you can then carry the rig with no problems at all. You only need a little room by the water where you can tune the rig, and after that you can quickly put the rig into the water. Look at the photographs and captions overleaf:

When carrying the mast, the mast foot must point towards the wind.

1. Place the board close to the water. The daggerboard is inserted and raised.
2. Hold the rig by mast and wishbone boom, and lift it above your head.
3. Take the rig to the water, with the mast foot still pointing towards the wind.
4. Put the rig into the water sufficiently far from the shore.
5. Only then place the board in the water; walk or paddle to the rig.
6. Insert the mast foot into the step. Attach the rig to the board with the leash.

Paddling with the sail extended

Frequently, there is not enough room near the bank to raise the sail undisturbed. Experience shows that the most crowded place is close by the shore where other boardsailors are setting out or coming back in, and children are playing about, swimming and diving by the water's edge. The best way of avoiding the hurly-burly in the shallows is to place the rig, fully extended, on the stern, leaving the mast foot in the step so that the rig is clear above the water. Paddle away, kneeling or lying on the board, until you are far enough from the shore to raise your rig safely. Alternatively you can unstep the mast foot and lie beneath the sail on top of the lower wishbone. It is easy to lift the sail slightly with your feet, and so keep it balanced.

Both of these methods of paddling with the rig extended are only suitable for light winds, however, but they can be useful if the wind falls light before you manage to reach the shore. This avoids your having to dismantle the rig on the water, and you can kneel or lie more comfortably on the board.

Opposite above left *With the mast foot pointing in to the wind . . .*
Opposite above right *. . . throw it over your head into the water.*
Opposite below left *Paddle your board to the rig . . .*
Opposite below right *. . . and fix the mast foot in the mast step.*

Below *Paddling with the rig extended.*

The way home

Before you actually sail away from the land, you must be absolutely sure that you know how to help yourself should your strength fail or the wind drop. Practise unrigging while you are on land; it is not so easy on the water. If you have any problems while on terra firma, you will find your difficulties increase when you are on an unsteady board, and you would therefore be wise to prepare yourself thoroughly by practising unrigging again when on the water close to the shore.

You can only paddle with the mast, whether standing or kneeling, if it is calm. This method is not advisable anyway when it is blowing because the rig has to be dismantled, and this takes too much time in an emergency, quite apart from the fact that something can so easily be lost. Without wanting to wish it on to anybody, the plain fact is that any-

Not as easy as it looks.

Paddling after unrigging.

International Distress Signal

one can find himself in a situation where he can no longer get back to shore under his own steam. There could be many reasons for this, varying from wrongly estimating the strength of the wind or one's own strength, or choosing the wrong sail, right up to failure of the gear.

Should it actually come to that point at some time, remember the basic rules of conduct above:

The distress signal illustrated below is internationally recognised in professional and sporting circles. The actions of raising your arms over your head and crossing them is an addition that has crept in with boardsailing.

- Keep calm and stay ON the board!
- Use the international distress signal to draw attention.
- If help does not come, do not wait too long before lying down on the board *without* the rig and paddling to the shore.

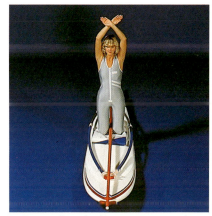

In Europe boardsailors cross arms.

I need help! Raise and . . . *lower your arms and stretch them sideways.*

Being towed

To prepare for a tow, lay your rig on the board, stowed as on p. 42. You can either hold on to the towing board's daggerboard strap or let yourself be pulled along, using your spare line as a towrope attached to the towing eye. It is easier still just to release the outhaul, fold the wishbone upwards and let the rig drag through the water close by the board (leave the mast foot in the step!). When being towed by a fast boat, be sure to remove the daggerboard because otherwise the board will heel over, or yaw wildly back and forth.

It is not enough just to watch others practising the technique of towing. Take the trouble to go out yourself with a friend and practise towing and being towed by each other on your sailboards.

Once you can tow your partner wherever you wish on the water, you will be ready for any emergency that might arise in the future. Being towed also works better after some practice.

Above *When being towed, hold on to the daggerboard strap.*
Below *Being towed with a towline.*
Opposite *Do not fail to practise towing and being towed.*

Climbing on to the board

In shallow water

The water should be at least knee deep. Climb aboard near the mast foot, that is to say, near the middle of the board; you can then support yourself with one hand on the board and the other on the mast. But take care: do not catch your fingers between the mast and the board! That can really hurt.

In deep water

When getting on to the board from deep water, you have to use your swimming skills to help you a bit.
 Place your hands flat on the centre of the board, to right and left of the mast, get some swing by lowering yourself rather deeper in the water, and pull your trunk on to the board. Make a powerful swimming stroke with your legs to push yourself out of the water, placing first one and then the other knee on the board.

Typical faults

It can be great fun trying to climb on board at the bow or the stern, but it takes a lot of energy and you do not always succeed.

Raising the sail — rig to leeward

Important advice

If you find after your first day's boardsailing that you have got cramp or even backache, the reason will be that you have been making mistakes when hauling the rig out of the water. For medical reasons, it is absolutely imperative to use the correct technique and a suitable rig, in order to avoid straining your spinal column. The two decisive points are to keep your back straight (that is the reason for the instruction 'head up'), and to start raising the sail with your knees bent. Using a smaller sail (an allround or medium sail) will also make it easier for you to raise the rig. Water runs off a smaller sail quicker when you pull it out of the water, and you present a smaller area of sail to the wind. This is the reason why boardsailing schools frequently use not just small sails but short booms too to help to make the rig lighter to hoist. The sail is easier to raise when it lies on the side of the board away from the wind, on the *lee* side. Leeward and lee mean the direction towards which the wind blows, while windward is the direction from which it blows. Before raising the sail you should find out where the wind is blowing from, for example, by looking at flags on shore or the direction of wind-raised waves, and relate wind direction to points on the shore.

Once you have raised the sail you have only to allow it to flutter freely for it to act as a wind direction indicator because the clew will always point downwind to leeward.

Feet a hand's breadth from the mast

Place your feet on the longitudinal axis of the board, to right and left of the mast foot and a hand's breadth from it. This is how you will feel steadiest. You can restrain the board from swinging round while you raise the sail by distributing your weight evenly between your feet.

The uphaul must reach right to the mast foot.

Starting position

The rig lies to leeward of the board, with the mast at right angles to the board. Your feet are a hand's breadth to right and left of the mast foot, your kees are bent, your trunk is upright, your back is straight and your head high. Grasp the lowest knot on the uphaul with both hands, and keep your arms straight.

Stretch your legs and raise the rig

At first, just straighten your legs to raise the rig slightly. Keep your back and arms straight. Having lifted it a little, wait for the water to run off which reduces weight. Lean back slightly to keep your balance.

Pull the rig clear of the water

Only now should you quickly pull the rig right out of the water by heaving on the uphaul, hand over hand.

Grasp the mast

Catch hold of the mast beneath the wishbone boom with one or both hands. Your arms are almost fully stretched, but the end of the boom must not be allowed to touch the water. Your knees are slightly bent, your trunk upright and your head up. The rig is now roughly at right angles to the board.

Shifting the sail from windward to leeward before raising it out of the water

Shifting the rig over the board from windward to leeward

The rig should always be lying to leeward when you are about to raise the sail. But if board and rig are left to themselves, even for a short time, or if you have fallen in to windward without letting go of the sail at the right moment, the rig will be on the wrong side of the board and there it will stay. A board floating on the water offers resistance to the wind

but virtually none to the water, whereas the opposite is true in the case of the rig. This lies in the water where the wind does not catch it, but it is braked by the water, and acts as if it were the board's sea anchor. The result is that, whatever its position, the board will swing around the sail until it is lying exactly at right angles to the wind. When you are standing on the board, this will happen more quickly because you increase the resistance to the wind.

When the rig is to windward like this it is extremely difficult to raise the rig, and so your first task is to shift the sail to the leeward side of the board. Generally beginners fall in when raising the rig to windward because the sail will hit you forcefully.

The following technique enables you to get the rig over to the lee side without risk. Drag the rig over the board mast first, either over the bow or the stern depending on which way the rig is lying. After some practice you will find that, when you do this quickly, the board will not turn but will stay across the wind. The difficult moment comes when your rig is lying on the board and is not in contact with the water; the board is then less steady, and it is best to get this wobbly stage over with quickly with a swing.

Above Raise the rig and drag it mast first towards the mast over the *bow*.
Below Raise the rig and drag it mast first towards the mast over the *stern*.

Above *Do not raise the rig until it is lying to leeward of the board.*

Shifting the rig from windward to leeward by turning the board

There is an easier way of getting into the correct starting position from which to raise the rig. You just raise the rig slightly by stretching your legs. The part of the sail that you bring out of the water by doing this offers more resistance to the wind than your body and the board combined; the board will then turn round until the rig is to windward. Although it takes longer to do it this way, you do not have problems over

Below *Raise the rig, let the wind drive it and turn it until there is a right angle between*

keeping your balance as part of the rig stays in the water, and there is always a right angle between rig and board. Little effort is needed provided you keep back and arms straight.

rig and board.

Common errors when raising the sail

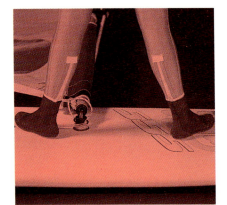

Feet are not equidistant a hand's breadth either side of the mast, and are not on the longitudinal axis of the board. It is hard to keep the board at right angles to the wind when you stand like this.

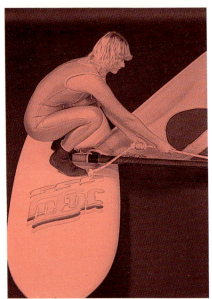

Low crouch. Feet are not flat on the board; the uphaul is grasped too high up; the sail cannot be raised this way.

Body not leaning back. Uphaul not held by the lowest knot. Spinal column in danger!

The sail has been pulled out of the water too quickly, and a fall to windward is the consequence!

Arms are bent and boom end is not close above the water. The rig does not help you to keep your balance.

Basic Position — Safety Position

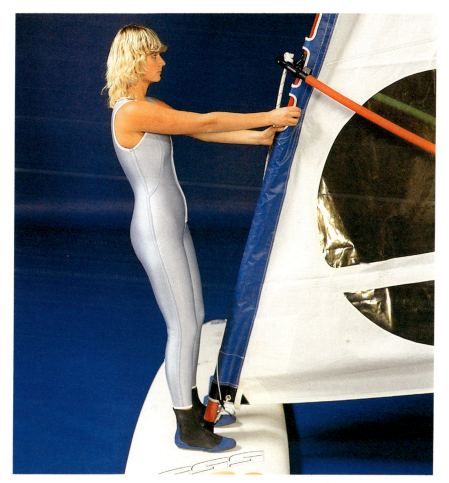

After you have raised the sail, you will feel steadiest if you:
■ keep your feet equidistant to left and right of the mast foot,
■ bend your knees slightly to keep your balance,
■ keep your head up and your back straight,
■ hold the mast with one or two hands,
■ keep your arms almost straight with the sail fluttering at right angles to the board and the boom end just out of the water.

This is the basic position; it is also a safety position, because you can have a good look round as you stand there, and get an idea of what is happening all around you. It is essential that you feel secure in this basic position before you continue with later exercises.

Above *The basic position provides even beginners with a sure stance.*
Below *Take a good look round when in the basic position.*

Moving through the water by swinging the rig

The basic position and exercises with the rig preparatory to moving off

If you swing the rig gently towards the bow or the stern, keeping your arms nearly straight as you do so, and lean slightly towards the wind, the sail will fill with wind for a few moments, and the pressure of the wind on the sail suffices to turn the board. This is how you keep the board in the correct position, with a right angle between rig and board. If you rake (tilt) the sail towards the stern and then bring it back to make a right angle again, the board will even start to sail. Your feet stay in the same position as you do this, to left and right of the mast foot. After practising a little, you will be able to sail a zig-zag course like this, and if there is an onshore wind you can keep clear of the land and even make towards a specific objective. That objective cannot, however, be exactly in the direction from which the wind is blowing, because this technique barely enables you to work towards the wind.

Rake the rig towards the bow, and the bow will turn away from the wind.

Rake the rig towards the stern, and the bow will turn towards the wind.

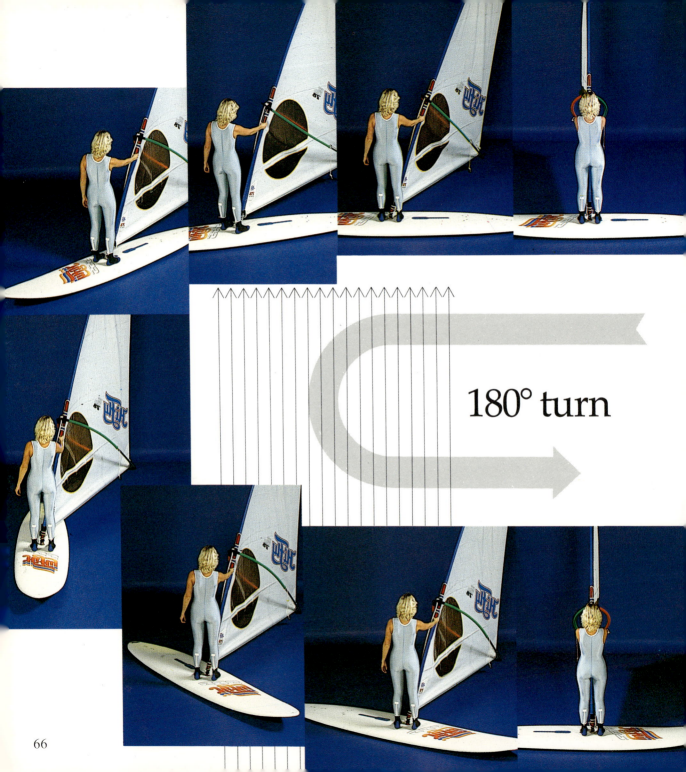

If you lean the rig into the wind and swing it over the stern, the board can be turned through a semi-circle.

From raking the rig to the 180° turn

Raking the rig when standing in the basic position is also good preparation for turning the board through 180°. The board then starts to move and will describe a semi-circle, but, more important, you can change the direction in which the board sails in this way. After turning a semi-circle you can return to the place from which you started.

The method is to rake the rig towards the stern, holding the mast with one or both hands. The sail fills with wind, the board gathers way, and the bow turns towards the wind.

Your feet must allow the board to turn, so lift them alternately and let the board turn beneath you. Keep your back towards the wind all the time that the board is turning.

The turn is complete when the bow is facing in exactly the opposite direction; you are back in a 'new' basic position with a right angle again between rig and board, and the end of the boom just above the water.

You can only turn the board like this, using the rig to make it swing round, if the end of the boom stays close to the water, so keep your arms straight enough for the rig to just avoid dipping into the water.

Obviously you can just as easily rake the sail towards the bow, but be warned that the board will drift rapidly while the sail is swinging over the bow. This is dangerous in an offshore wind, because the board will be blown rapidly away from the shore and possibly out to sea. You then run the risk that you will not have enough strength left to get back to land under your own steam.

If you turn by raking the sail towards the bow rather than to the stern when an onshore wind is blowing, the board will be driven back on to the shore.

Rake the sail towards the bow; the bow will turn away from the wind. Rake the rig towards the stern: the bow will turn towards the wind.

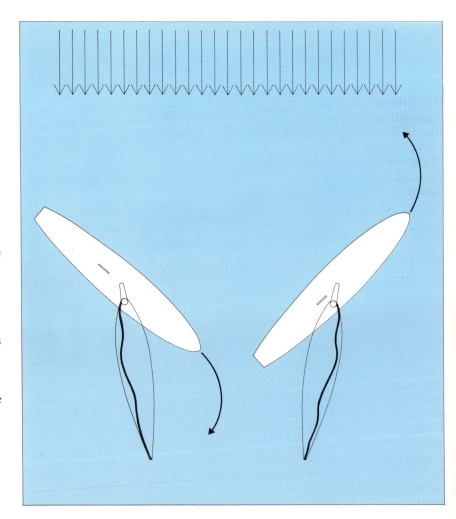

68

If you are not sure that you can turn your board towards the direction you want to sail in, you should not attempt to start out, however great the temptation, because returning home always involves turning the board round 180°.

This is the correct way: lift your feet alternately so that the board can turn beneath them. Keep your back turned towards the wind.

If the turn does not come off, the following faults are usually the reason:

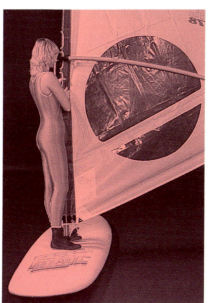 

The mast is upright, the boom end is not close above the water; consequently the board will not turn. Watch out – it is barely possible to avoid falling over backwards now!

Feet left in the basic position while the board turns. The mast comes up against your shin; consequently the board cannot turn further.

69

Right of way between craft

Even someone who has never had anything to do with water transport, on looking at the photograph opposite, will decide correctly who is well advised to give way. Yet although the difference in size of the ferry boat and the group of boardsailors is impressive and convincing, the size of the vessels plays little part where rights of way on the water are concerned. There are rules called the collision regulations ('actually international regulations for prevention of collision at sea'); these are not the same, by the way, as right of way rules in racing.

A 'sailing vessel' may not impede the passage of a vessel which can safely navigate only within a narrow channel or fairway.

> Boardsailors should always stay well clear of large motor vessels, and not just at times when the regulations say they must. When a large vessel is close by, her wind shadow and suction can be deadly dangerous. A ship of this sort of size cannot 'brake' even when the engine order 'full speed astern' is given. A boardsailor would barely be noticed, and anyway the ship would be unable to avoid him or come to a halt; her stopping distance will be several hundreds of metres.

The rule for most other water craft is: you cannot brake on the water; instead you must take avoiding action. Because it is virtually impossible to stop quickly, as you can by braking hard in a motor car, you must know the right of way rules thoroughly and abide by them. The important difference from road traffic regulations is that, on the water, while the vessel without right of way has to give way, the vessel with right of way has to maintain her course and speed. If vessels sailing towards each other both altered course simultaneously in the same direction, a collision could be inevitable and this is why the right of way vessel must not alter her course while the vessel whose duty it is to give way takes action to avoid a collision. Obviously you may not enforce your right of way; possibly the other vessel may not have seen you, or may not know the rules. Even if you have right of way, you may have to alter course in an emergency if the other vessel has failed to do so when there is a danger of collision. If you are in any doubt, shout loudly to draw the other vessel's attention to the fact that it is his duty to give way. If that does not help, give way yourself or stop your board (see p. 86). If it is your duty to give way, you must alter course in good time and so clearly that the other person can see what you are doing, and so avoid any misunderstandings.

> The basic rules when giving way are:
> early action
> decisive action
> obvious action

1. Power gives way to sail

Unfortunately people in motor boats, and those who are in a sailing boat which is being propelled by its auxiliary engine, forget now and then that they must give way to vessels that are propelled only by sails. The rule is sensible because a boat under power is easier to control, whether the wind is strong or light. But do not rely too much on the rule and never enforce your right of way – you could get the worst of it if you did.

2. Muscle power gives way to sail

Boats propelled by people paddling, rowing or pedalling, that is to say boats propelled by muscle power, have to give way to a boardsailor, but naturally it is only sensible not to assume that people who are enjoying their leisure like this know the rules of the road on the water. You, on your sailboard, will soon be so manoeuvrable that you will be able to stop without difficulty, and alter course if you find, say, that a man rowing does not react to a friendly shout. Whenever possible you should give way to racing rowing boats, because it is very difficult for them to stop or alter course sharply.

3. Right of way rules when sailing vessels meet

a) Port tack gives way to starboard tack

To understand this rule you must first know that the two sides of your sailboard have different names, just as do those of a ship. When you look ahead over the bow, the left side of the board is the port side and the right side is the starboard side. At night ships show red and green side lights to port and starboard respectively.

Below left *Top: on port tack.   Bottom: on starboard tack.*
Below right *Port tack: Give way by luffing (A), stopping by backing the sail (B), or with a stop gybe (C).*
Starboard tack: Do not alter course.

The term starboard tack applies to a board (or boat) when the sail is on the left or port side of the board and the wind comes from starboard, whereas the board is on port tack

> If two vessels under sail meet, the one that has its sail to port (the starboard tack boat), has the right of way over the board with its sail to starboard.

when the wind blows from the port side and the sail is to starboard.

The boardsailor on port tack *must* give way, while the starboard tack boardsailor must maintain his course.

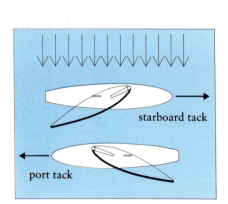

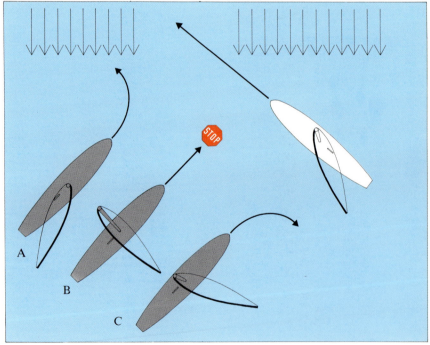

b) Windward gives way to leeward
When vessels or boards are on the same tack so that 'starboard' no longer applies, the leeward before windward rule is the right of way rule. This, in theory, benefits the vessel that is in the 'more adverse' situation. It is harder to sail to windward, towards the direction from which the wind is blowing, than to sail downwind, to leeward.

If two sailors or boardsailors have their sails on the same side of the board (both to port or both to starboard), then the boat or board which is to leeward of the other has right of way, and may maintain its course.

The leeward side of your sailboard is the side where your clew is when you are under way: windward is the opposite side. You have a clear view to windward but you have to look through the window in your sail or to one side of the sail if you want to look round the water to leeward. As vessels being sailed to leeward of you will have right of way when they are

Leeward before windward.

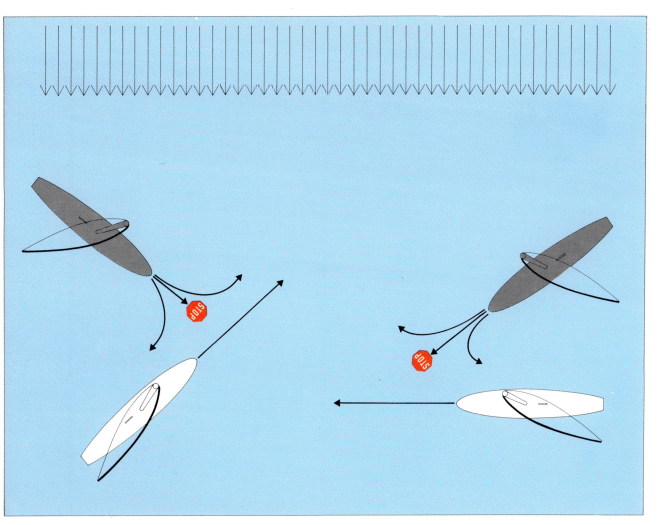

on the same tack, you must keep a particularly sharp lookout in this area.

c) Overtaker keeps clear
If you are sailing faster than a vessel ahead can, you overtake her, on either side (see p. 99) but you must avoid hindering or endangering her.

For a boardsailor, that means at least two mast lengths away, which is about 10 m (over 10 yds).

The other boardsailor would then be clear of danger if a sudden gust caused you to fall in or drop the sail.

Above *Keep a safe distance away.*
Below *When possible, overtake to windward so that you avoid being blanketed.*
Opposite *In a race start on starboard tack.*

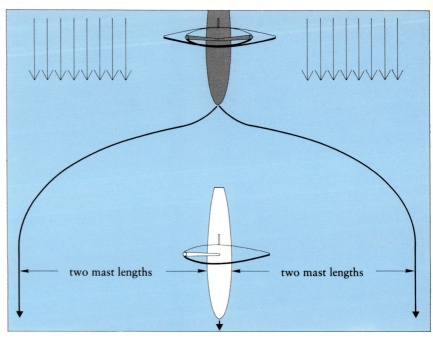

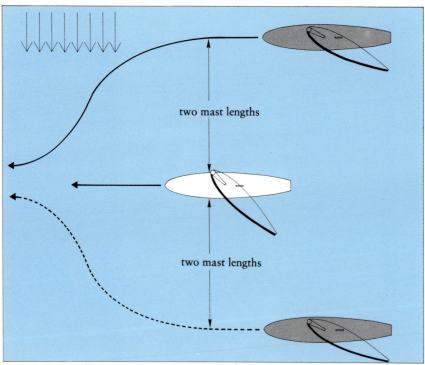

Recommendations on how to behave in busy waters

1. Before starting, before every alteration of course, and before tacking or gybing, check whether the water is clear in your direction. Anticipate what other people are planning.
2. While under way, look ahead to where you are going, but also check frequently by looking right round to find out what is happening nearby.
3. Especially when near the shore, watch out for swimmers and divers, and give way clearly and in good time.

Remember to allow for the length of your mast, which is almost 5 m long (a good 16 ft).

Starting

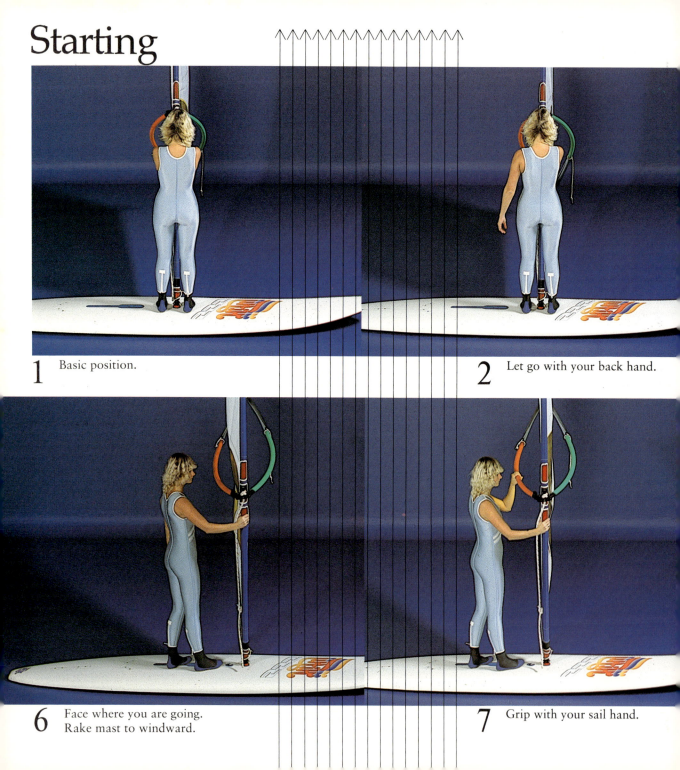

1 Basic position.

2 Let go with your back hand.

6 Face where you are going. Rake mast to windward.

7 Grip with your sail hand.

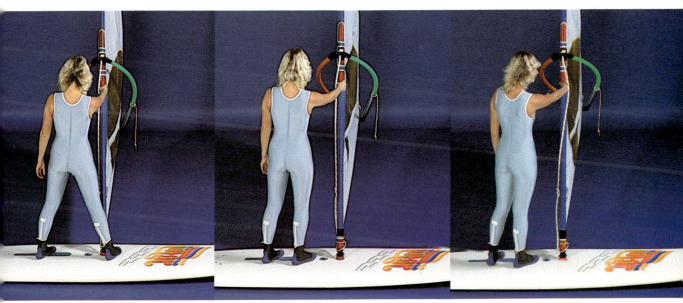

3 Back foot further behind the mast.

4 Front foot behind the mast.

5 Wishbone boom end over the water at 90°.

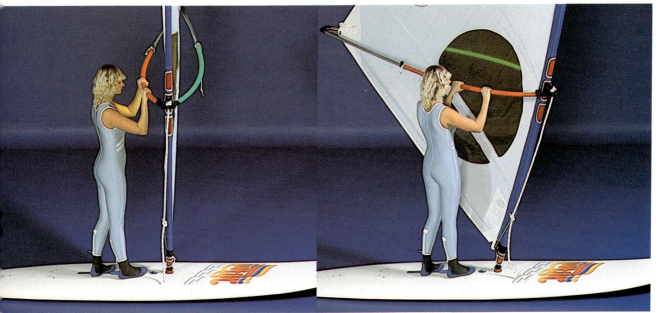

8 Grip with your mast hand.

9 Turn your trunk back again.

Practising balancing the rig

You can play about practising this most important element of the starting procedure either on the water or on land where you have no problems over balancing. You will soon find out how far to windward you have to pull the rig with your mast hand in order to get it balanced and upright. Once you have discovered this, you will be able to do all that is illustrated straight off, and you will soon realise that in a strong wind the rig has to be raked considerably further to windward if it is to stay balanced. This is important when it comes to starting in a strong wind.

Preparing to start

Getting under way can be broken down into two quite separate sections: preparing to start and actually starting. Preparation includes altering your stance on the board, changing your grip and taking a good look all round the water.

A slight pause before setting off enables you to check your starting position:
■ Your feet must both be aft of the mast, parallel to each other and at an oblique angle to the longitudinal axis of the board.
■ The rig is tilted towards the water, with the end of the boom just above the surface.
■ The angle between rig and board is about 90°.

Starting

The decisive point in the sequence of movements which precedes gathering way is to pull the sail so far to windward (towards the wind) with your front (mast) hand, by turning your shoulder, that the rig becomes 'light' and will balance unsupported for a short time. In most cases, a start fails simply because the boardsailor too quickly interrupts this raking of the rig to windward by prematurely catching hold of the boom with his back hand.

The sequence of individual movements when starting is as follows:
■ Check that the water ahead of the bow is clear in the direction in which you will be sailing.
■ With your mast hand on the mast, turn your forward shoulder to pull the rig to windward until it becomes quite light. The end of the boom will then generally be pointing obliquely upwards, while the angle between board and rig remains 90°.
■ With your sail hand (nearer the stern), catch hold of the boom in front of your shoulder.
■ In the same way, grasp the boom with your mast hand. The distance between your hands on the boom should be about the breadth of your shoulders. Let your elbows hang slack. There is still no pressure in the sail, which is fluttering.
■ In order to start sailing, turn your shoulders back without altering the angle of your arms until the sail stops fluttering near the luff, just behind the mast. Place your weight on your back leg by leaning back slightly. Look where you are going.

Waiting position

You can practise getting under way several times in succession by pulling the rig to windward until it is balanced, and grasping the boom with sail and mast hands; this is the waiting position. You can then practise starting as often as you like.

When you turn your trunk back while keeping your arms at the same angle, pressure on the sail makes the board start to move. Turning your trunk forward takes the pressure out of the sail again, and the board slows down.

Turning your trunk back is called 'hardening in' or 'sheeting in' the sail, while turning to face further forward is called 'easing' or 'sheeting out' the sail. Your shoulders remain parallel to the wishbone boom as you turn, and your arms stay bent at the same angle.

If you can spend some time in the waiting position with the rig balanced, you will find it much easier to start afterwards.

Left *Rig to windward – turn your shoulder forward: no pressure in the sail means no, or only slow, motion through the water.*
Right *Turn the trunk back while keeping the elbows bent at the same angle: pressure in the sail means gathering way means sailing position.*

Starting position

Starting preparations are complete when you are in the starting position:
- with feet behind the mast, turned forwards at an angle,
- slightly bent knees, ready to move,
- mast hand holding the mast,
- 90° angle between rig and board,
- boom end above the water,
- looking where you are going.

Most faults are in the starting position itself, or are made when actually starting.

Below left Rig not at right angles, mast pulled too close to the body.
Above right Rig not at right angles, mast too far towards the bow, and held too far from the body.
Below right Rig too far from the body.

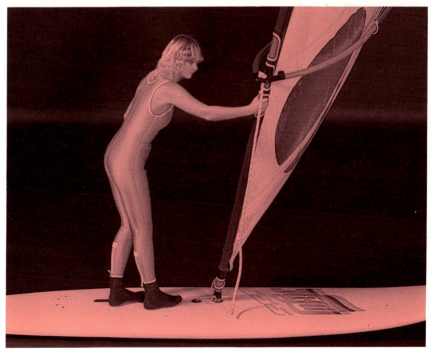

83

Starting

- Rig to windward.
- Take hold with sail hand and mast hand.
- Gather way.

Above left Rig too close to the body.
Above right Rig not at right angles. Mast pulled too close to the body.
Below left Rig not far enough to windward.
Below right The most common error: the front arm is straightened when gathering way, hips are bent, and the sail hangs to leeward.

At the start: rig to windward until it is balanced.

Stand some way behind the mast.

Emergency Stop

You become part of the traffic the very first time that you start in open water. You must know and abide by the rules of the road, and be careful to control your board so well that you can bring it to a rapid halt at any moment. There is an effective but not very elegant way of doing this.

In good time, drop your rig quickly to leeward and use all your weight to force it down into the water. All you need is sufficient room to leeward, and you will of course have to make the effort to pull the sail up out of the water again afterwards.

A slightly more difficult technique is to brake your speed with the rig upright by turning your shoulders so far forward that the wind strikes the wrong side of the sail. The sail is then said to be aback.

When you make an emergency stop by backing the sail, you press hard against the rig, holding it as if you were pushing a truck. If you continue to back the sail, the bow will turn beneath it. Continuing the emergency stop by turning the board to face the opposite way is called a stop gybe (see Gybing, p. 106).

Left *Turn shoulder forward: reduction in speed.*
Centre *Lean forward and hold the sail aback: stop.*
Right *Turn shoulder back: gather way.*

Do not try to enforce your right of way. If the other man does not react to your shout, make an emergency stop.

Points of sailing

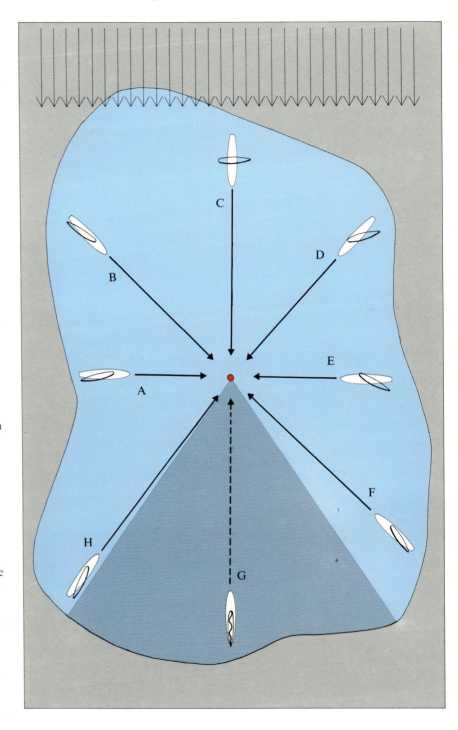

The diagram shows a number of boardsailors who are all trying to sail the shortest course from the banks of a lake to the buoy in the middle. A and E are on a point of sailing with which you will be familiar right from the start. The wind is blowing at right angles to them, and they are on a beam reach.

Points of sailing further to leeward of a beam reach are broad reaching and running. Boardsailors B and D are on a broad reach, and boardsailor C, with the wind blowing from dead behind him, is on the point of sailing called a run. When closer to the wind than a beam reach, the boards sail into the wind. Board F is said to be on a close reach. And what of G? He is lying in an area from which it is impossible to sail straight to the buoy because a board cannot sail directly into the wind, but only at a more or less acute angle towards it. Board H is sailing at that angle, which is very close to the wind, and is said to be close-hauled or on the wind.

As you sail towards the wind you work to windward, whereas when broad reaching and running you sail downwind to leeward. Ground gained to windward does not mean

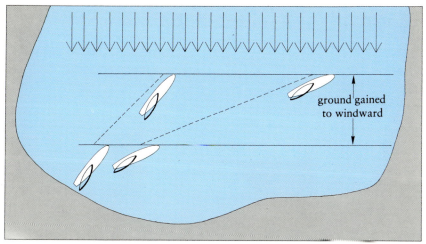

the distance that you have covered over the water but the distance between two imaginary lines at right angles to the wind direction, one through your starting position and the other through your position at that specific moment.

Below *Reaching, the fastest point of sailing.*

Altering course — how to steer

BEAR AWAY – to sail farther away from the wind – to point less high.

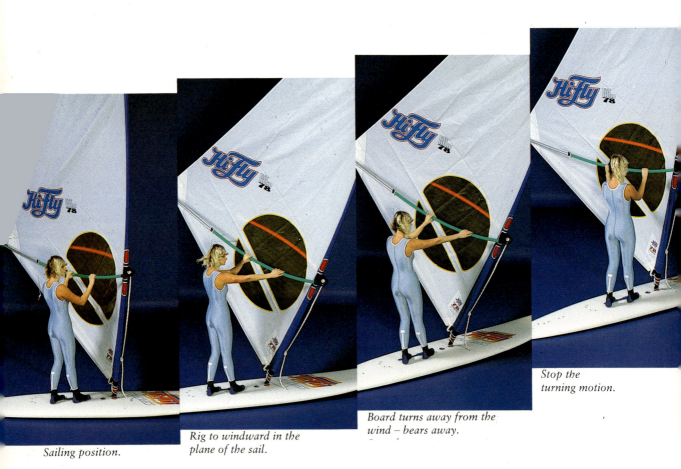

Sailing position.

Rig to windward in the plane of the sail.

Board turns away from the wind – bears away.

Stop the turning motion.

When bearing away, rake (tilt) the rig to windward along the plane of the sail, towards the mast, by stretching your forward arm.

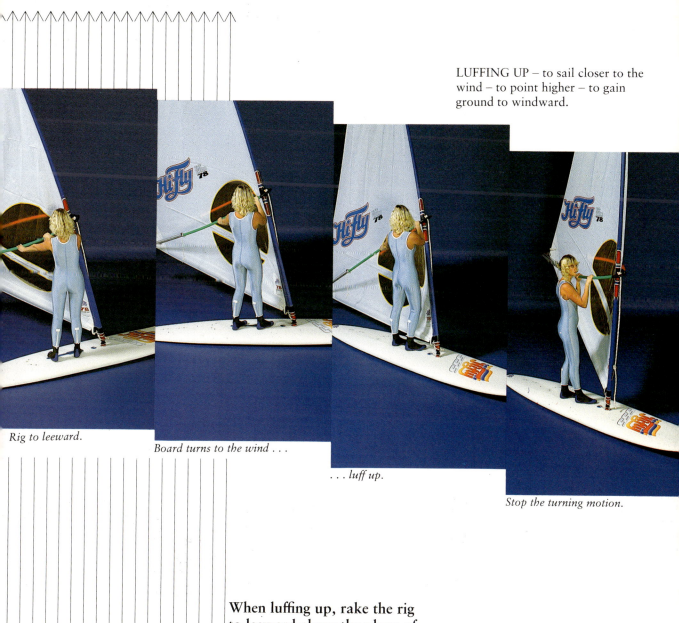

LUFFING UP – to sail closer to the wind – to point higher – to gain ground to windward.

Rig to leeward.

Board turns to the wind . . .

. . . luff up.

Stop the turning motion.

When luffing up, rake the rig to leeward along the plane of the sail, towards the end of the boom, by stretching your back arm.

91

Steering in practice

How do you steer a sailboard? First you need an explanation of the way you describe a change of direction when steering. There is no problem when driving a car; you turn to left or right when you go round left- or right-hand corners. These words are familiar and self-explanatory, but they cannot be used on the water because, when sailing, everything is governed by the wind, and that includes altering course.

> The terms used when altering course state whether you will be sailing closer to the wind, in which case you luff up, or whether you will be sailing further away from the wind, when you bear away.
> Luff = turn towards the wind.
> Bear away = turn away from the wind.

You will understand why these very different terms make sense on the water when you look at the boards in the diagram below, both of which are turning right. When boardsailor A turns right, he turns away from the wind – he bears away – whereas when sailor B turns right, he sails closer to the wind – he luffs up.

The action you take in order to luff up is exactly opposite to your action when you wish to bear away.

The most effective action when altering course is to rake the mast in

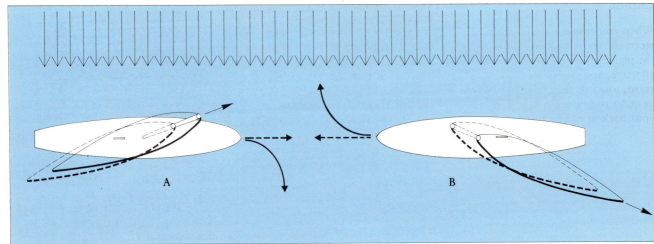

Above Both boardsailors are turning right. Boardsailor A rakes his rig to windward to do this, while boardsailor B rakes his rig to leeward.
Right Raking the rig in the plane of the sail: the plane of the sail is defined by the three corners of the sail. The chord is a cross-section through the plane of the sail parallel to the boom, in the diagram the line between mast and clew (end of the wishbone boom). Raking the rig in the plane of the sail means that you tilt the sail in the direction of the extension of the chord of the sail to windward or to leeward.

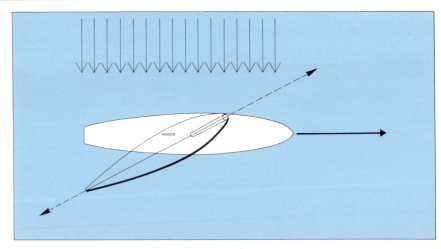

the plane of the sail to windward (towards the mast) or to leeward (towards the end of the boom). While you are doing this, the sail must stay in the same position relative to the wind (in the same plane), and whatever you do you must not let it flutter. The rig is raked to windward (mast direction) in the plane of the sail to make the board bear away, and to leeward (boom end direction) when luffing up.

Luffing up

When you rake the rig in order to steer, the movement has to be along the plane of the sail to be really effective, and you move it to leeward, towards the end of the boom in order to luff up. Just stretch out your back arm, and the board will begin to curve round towards the wind. As a general rule, it is important that, when you are altering course, and particularly when luffing, your course should be straight and steady both before and after turning. The way you do this is to complete the action made with the rig to alter course by deliberately stopping the turning motion; you rake the rig back again to the position it was in before luffing so that the board sails straight ahead with the boom parallel to the water again. Having initiated luffing by raking the rig, it is important to stop the board from swinging round too far, because almost all boards are very sensitive and react so quickly that the tendency is to stop luffing too late. The wind then strikes the wrong side of the sail, and pushes both you and the rig into the water.

Bearing away

To make the board react as quickly as possible to your steering action by turning away from the wind and bearing away, you rake the rig to windward in the plane of the sail. You do this by stretching out your front arm and pulling your back hand towards your head.

> Be careful not to let the sail shake and lift forward near the mast, and be sure that the board is lying absolutely flat on on the water.

If your weight is wrong on the board and you immerse one edge, you may find that the turning motion is accelerated, but sometimes the opposite occurs and you find suddenly that the board keeps sailing straight ahead even though you have used your arms correctly. This is because, by tilting the board, you have caused the forces acting on the underwater part of the board to neutralise the effect of your steering action with the rig (see The theory of steering, p. 95).

Tight turning by shifting weight and loading the side of the board.

Bad steering causes catapulting

Even if a catapult fall is the result of incorrect sailing, it is still one of the most exciting boardsailing experiences. The feeling of free flight is not easily forgotten. If you wish to avoid a catapult, or to provoke it, watch out for the following faults:
- when bearing away, one foot is forward of the mast
- trunk is bent forward
- sail is hardened right in to the longitudinal axis of the board

Very soon afterwards (depending on your weight and the wind strength), invisible forces will whip you up, and you will suddenly find yourself momentarily enjoying the pleasure of weightlessness. Should you become disorientated and wonder where you are going to come down, at least protect your head!

Above *Demonstration of a catapult fall: Randy Naish.*
Below left *Right: Foot ahead of the mast. Mast not far enough to windward when bearing away.*
Right *Far right: Hips bent. The mast has also been raked forward towards the bow rather than to windward.*

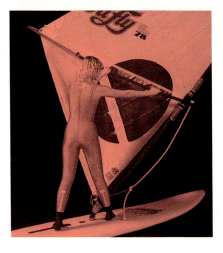 

The theory of steering

Sailing boats are steered with a rudder, but a sailboard has no such turnable fin at the stern. A sailboard can nevertheless be steered very exactly.

The following facts, which are concerned with the effect of forces acting on board and sail, are very much simplified, but they will help to explain the principles by which a board is steered.

A force is generated when wind flows over a sail, and this force can be said to be centred at a point on the sail called the *centre of effort* (CE), which lies somewhere above the boom in the area where the camber of the sail is greatest.

The actual *position* of the CE depends both on the size and outline shape of the sail, and on sail camber, that is to say, on how deep the camber is and where the fullness of the sail lies.

The *direction of sail force*, broadly speaking, acts at right angles to the chord of the sail; the chord is the imaginary line which connects the luff to the clew at boom level.

Resistance acts on those parts of the sailboard that are submerged, and the centre at which these forces act is called the *centre of lateral resistance* (CLR) which, in the case of an all-round board, lies somewhere near the daggerboard. The actual *position* of the board's CLR at a given moment is governed by all the submerged parts – especially the daggerboard and fin(s) – and on where the sailor is standing.

The *direction* of the resistance force is exactly opposite to the direction of the forces acting on the sail. When sailing straight ahead sail force (F_S) and resistance (R) lie on a common line.

The way to steer the sailboard is to move the two forces in relation to each other, this causes a turning force to arise. The size of this turning force depends on the sizes of sail force and resistance, and on the distance between the lines of action of these forces.

There are two ways of altering course. Steering with the sail is the general rule; sail force is shifted by raking the rig. Experienced boardsailors can also steer by shifting their weight back towards the stern, or by deliberately submerging one side of the board, in other words, by steering with the board. This moves the

A sailboard sails straight on any point of sailing when the lines of action of sail force (F_S) and resistance (R) are in direct opposition. (CE = Centre of effort and CLR = Centre of lateral resistance.)

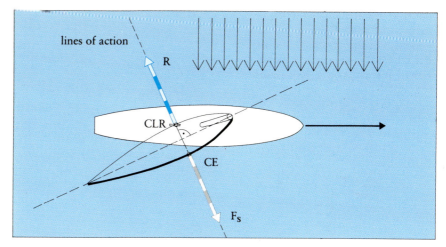

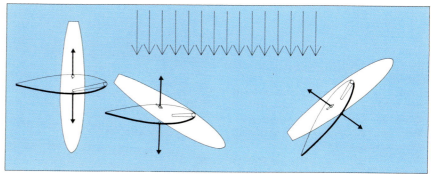

centre of lateral resistance, and is particularly effective at higher speeds, which is why it is best to steer with the board in strong winds.

The two ways of altering course can be used together, but this calls for a lot of practice and the first essential is to be able to steer competently with the rig. This book only covers rig steering.

An important point here is that when you are practising you must be careful to keep your board flat on the water as you sail, because pressing down either side will provoke an unwanted reaction from the board. If you submerge the sides of an all-round board with a long daggerboard in order to alter course, forcing down the side of the board which will be outside as you turn will encourage and speed up the turn, whereas putting weight on the inside edge slows or prevents the turning motion. To summarise steering methods:

Rig steering:
Water force constant, sail force shifted.

Board steering:
Sail force constant, water force shifted.

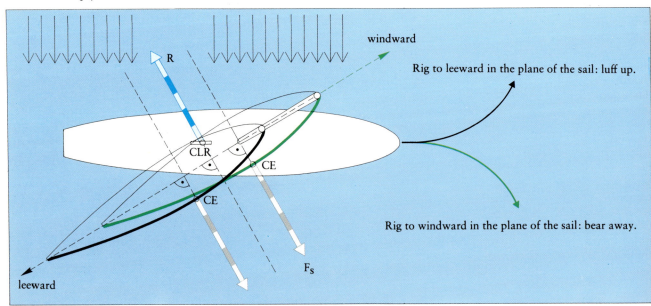

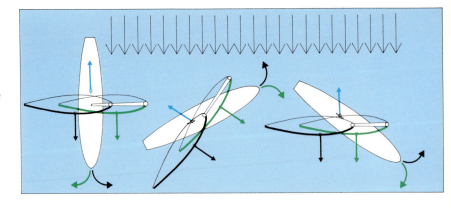

Steering with the rig. The lines of action of sail force (F_S) and resistance (R) no longer coincide. A turning moment arises between the points where resistance and sail force act. The turning moment initiated by raking the rig will be greatest when the rig is raked at right angles to the line of action of sail force and resistance, which means in the plane of the sail.

How does the sail work?

The importance of sail camber

You learned when rigging the sail that it has to be extended with the downhaul and the outhaul; altering the tension on these two lines makes the sail take up the desired shape. The efficiency of a sail is determined not only by its size and outline shape, but, in particular, by the position and depth of camber. The point where camber is deepest must be nearer the luff than the clew of a sailboard's sail, and the depth of camber should be about an eighth of the sail chord length. The sail in the figure below is cut flat, and maximum camber clearly lies forward of the centre of the sail. Such a sail is manageable and can be pulled out of the water easily; it is therefore particularly suitable for beginners.

The importance of the angle of attack

Your sail will not draw with optimum efficiency unless it is absolutely full of wind with the luff just not lifting; it will then be set correctly or, to put it in physics terminology, the angle between wind direction and the chord of the sail (the angle of attack) will be correct. The angle of attack will be between 15° and 20°, depending on the degree of camber of the sail.

You must be careful to keep the angle of attack just right, because it is this that ensures you use least effort and sail at maximum speed.

You can easily check that your sail is at the correct angle to the wind by sheeting it in just far enough for it not to lift at the luff. First sheet out your sail until it starts to lift (shake) close by the mast, and then harden it until the shaking stops (see Starting and Waiting position, p. 80). Your sail will develop maximum sail force when you keep it in this borderline state between full and lifting.

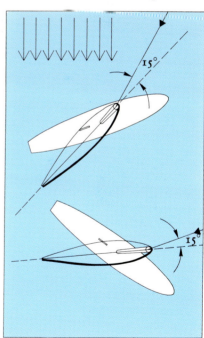

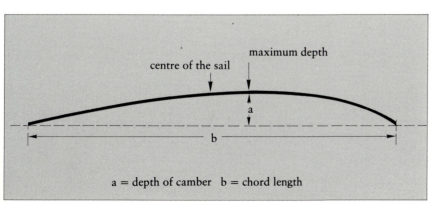

Above *Angle of attack: angle between sail chord and the direction of the wind used for sailing.*
Left *Section with camber about 40% along the length of the chord and maximum depth about 12%.*

Airflow over the sail

In order to grasp the connection between sail camber, angle of attack and sail force, you must first realise that wind, which you use as your driving force when boardsailing, is moving air.

Strictly speaking, air is made up of tiny particles which each have a certain mass and inertia. They have the property of maintaining their direction and speed provided that they do not meet an obstacle.

If you set your sail across the wind, these air particles come up against the sail and force it in the same direction as the wind is blowing (see diagram) in just the same way as the wind blows leaves away. You do not even need a sail in order to make progress; any flat and reasonably large object would be equally effective. But this statement is true only when you are talking about travelling exactly downwind. It is quite different when you are planning to sail across the wind, or even at an angle towards it.

Look at the top drawing on p. 99. The streamlines indicate the paths of individual air particles within the air stream. At a certain distance from the sail they flow past the windward and leeward sides of the sail without hindrance. Unlike the sail set across the wind, they are not deflected in all directions where they meet the sail, but are diverted into paths which follow the camber of the sail for some way. The deflection caused by the curvature of the sail has the effect of accelerating the particles which are on the lee side of the sail, and decelerating those to windward. As pressure in a stream is governed by its speed (the faster the stream the

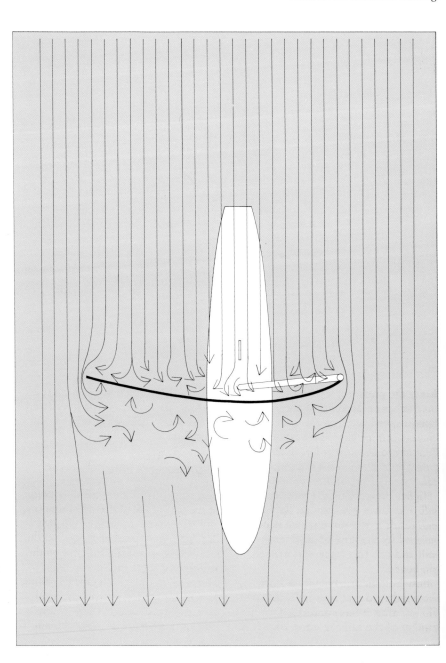

Wind on the sail when running.

Below left *Pressure is lower to leeward than to windward. The pressure difference at the sail makes the board move.*

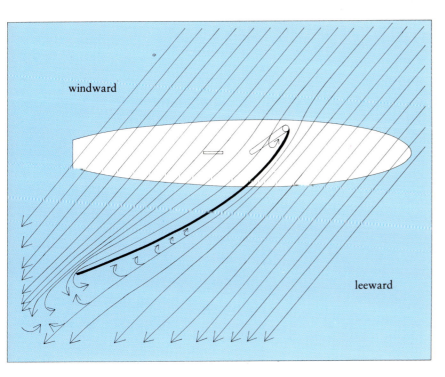

lower the pressure) a pressure difference arises on account of the variation in speed between the windward (faster) and leeward (slower) sides. *Pressure to leeward is lower than pressure to windward*; the sail is in effect *sucked to windward*.

Higher pressure on the windward side and lower pressure on the lee side result in the force which is developed by the flow of air over the sail, and it is this force that propels the board.

Flow becomes turbulent on both the windward and leeward sides of the sail after it has conformed to the camber of the sail for some way. It is only some distance beyond the sail that the air particles flow in ordered streamlines again without turbulence.

Blanketing – wind shadow

The zone of turbulent air downwind of the sail is called the wind shadow, and the extent of the area affected depends, among other things, on the size and shape of the sail and on the strength of the wind. If you want to overtake another sailboard by sailing past to leeward, you have to avoid its wind shadow, otherwise you will lose your wind when you are blanketed by the sailboard to windward. Similarly if you are being overtaken by a board to windward, you should expect to be blanketed by the overtaker as he sails past. Pressure on your sail is reduced so suddenly that it can make you fall into the water to windward. You will avoid these problems if you leave a distance of at least two mast lengths between yourself and the vessel to windward when you are overtaking and also be complying with the right of way rules (see p. 74).

Lateral force and driving force

When discussing steering, it was pointed out that air flow over the whole length of the sail exerts a total sail force which acts at the centre of effort. On most points of sailing only part of this force is converted into driving force. Total force is the result of two forces, one acting in the direction of board motion, the other at right angles to the board. The former, driving force, causes the board

Below *Blanketing.*

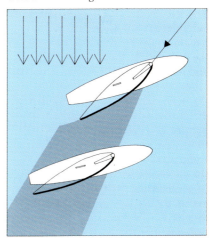

to move forward (upper diagram) while the latter, lateral force tries to push the board to leeward of the direction of motion. You can often steer directly towards an objective initially, but then find that you do not reach it on account of the lateral force (centre diagram).

The angle between the course sailed through the water and the direction in which the bow points is called leeway, and the effect of leeway on your course varies with the strength of the wind and the underwater shape of your board.

The important point, therefore, is how and why the two forces in this parallelogram of forces shift to favour driving force or lateral force, because naturally what you need is a higher proportion of driving force from any given value of total force.

The ratio of driving force to lateral force does not so much depend on the point of sailing as on how the

Above F_T = total sail force; F_R = driving force; F_S = lateral force; R = resistance. Centre *Leeway*. Below *The closer that the sail has to be sheeted, the greater will lateral force (F_S) be and therefore the smaller will driving force (F_R) be.*

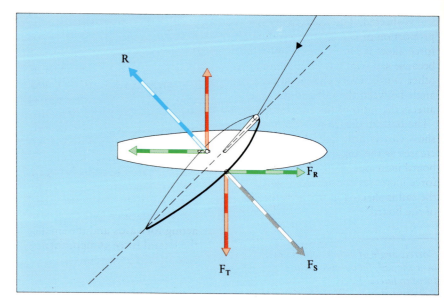

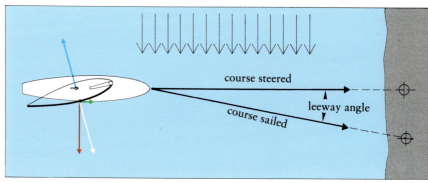

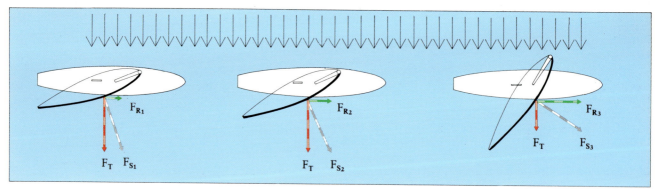

sail is sheeted. The reason why the proportion of driving force to lateral force alters is purely and simply because sail trim has been altered; in other words, every change in the angle between the sail and the board affects the ratio of the two forces.

The bottom diagrams on p. 100 show clearly how lateral force decreases as the angle between sail and board increases. Conversely lateral force increases considerably when the sail is sheeted in towards the side of the board.

Correct angle of attack: optimum airflow over the sail, favourable ratio of driving force to lateral force.
Sail sheeted in too close. Airflow breaks away, total force (F_T) is reduced and the proportion of lateral force (F_S) is large, as is leeway.
Sail sheeted out too far. The sail is aback at the luff. The forward third of the sail is not drawing, sail force (F_T) shifts towards the clew, and the board luffs up.

In practice this means that:

> The closer you have to sheet in the sail to the side of the board in order to maintain the correct angle of attack and optimum airflow, the greater will lateral force be, and so will leeway.
>
> Correspondingly, the more you increase the angle between sail and board to get the sail to draw properly, the greater the proportion of driving force acting forwards and the smaller the lateral force component; leeway will be reduced.

If you do not trim your sail properly to the wind, the direction of sail force and the ratio of driving force to lateral force will be affected. If a sail is sheeted in too close (too large an angle of attack) the effect will be that airflow will break away very early from the lee side of the sail. Suction is reduced and, with that, the power produced by the sail. Furthermore, lateral force increases on account of the unfavourable direction in which sail force acts.

The forward third of a sail that is sheeted out too far (too small an angle of attack) will shake and may even back, and in both cases there will be a noticeable loss of speed. The value of total sail force depends on maintaining optimum airflow over the sail (correct angle of attack), and it is this that is decisive when it comes to board speed. Furthermore, when a sail is wrongly trimmed and airflow is less than optimum, the position of the centre of effort at which the forces act also moves. When the angle of attack is too small, the board will tend to come up into the wind, whereas if it is too large, the result may be a catapult fall (see Steering, p. 94).

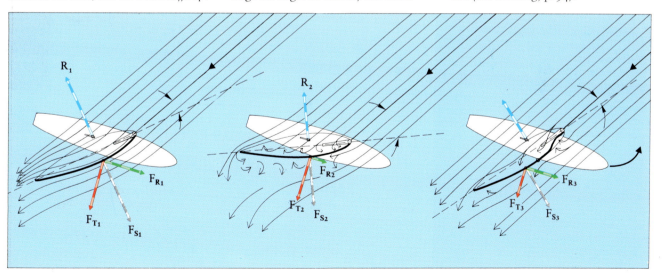

Tacking and gybing

The techniques that you have learnt so far enable you to get by on the water. You can raise the sail, start, sail forward and steer. If you want to get back to your starting point, you can manage with a 180° turn, but the 180° really is laborious because you have to stop first. Now, by learning how to tack and gybe, you will learn how you can turn round to sail back in the opposite direction without coming to a halt.

You are already familiar with the basic elements of tacking and gybing, namely luffing up and bearing away, and can do a 180° turn swinging the sail over stern or bow.

Tacking

If you tack several times when close-hauled, you are said to be beating. For safety reasons, you should spend a lot of time practising beating to windward by pointing high on the wind and tacking (also called going about); you will then be able to get back to the shore even when the wind is blowing from the land.

As you tack, you not only change the sail from one side to the other, but also gain ground to windward. Problems arise when tacking if you do not luff far enough and, having taken a step forward of the mast, fail to keep the turning momentum going until you are back in a 'new' basic position. Your board then starts to drift astern, and you will have failed to gain ground to windward.

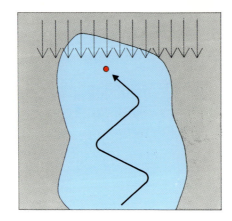

Above When several tacks follow each other in succession the term used is beating.
Below When tacking, the bow turns through the wind and the sail is swung over the stern.

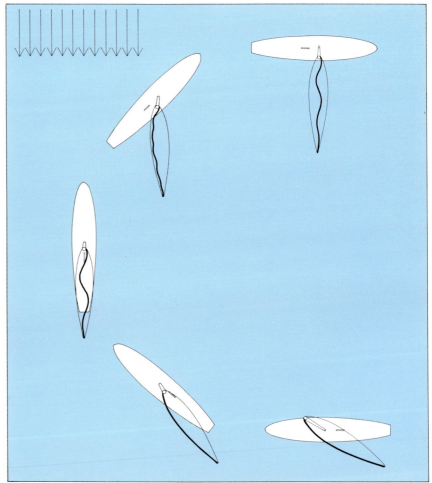

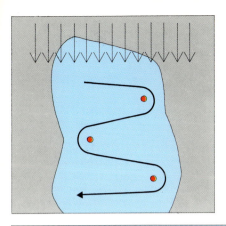

Above *In order to round the buoys as sketched, you have to gybe.*
Below *When gybing, the stern turns through the wind, and the sail is swung over the bow.*
A combination of tacking and gybing is needed to sail in a complete circle.

Gybing

This is really the most attractive manoeuvre when boardsailing, perhaps just because of the time it takes for you to feel really steady on the board – and you must be really steady if you are able to gybe in strong, as well as light, winds without constantly falling in.

Once you have gybed successfully, you will find it is much easier than tacking, and above all is more fun. And yet you can manage to spend all day boardsailing almost without needing to gybe.

You most need to gybe when you have to bear away beyond a dead run in order to give way to a vessel in restricted waters, or when some particular problem arises. Imagine, for example, that you want to sail down a long narrow lake, rounding buoys laid alternately either side. When you put your idea into practice and sail a zigzag course from one side of the lake to the other and back, you will gybe each time that you change direction.

In lighter winds, it is considerably easier to gybe than to tack because you do not have to step round the mast. You will find from experience that, in stronger winds, it is the bearing away that is most difficult, and the typical errors made are covered in the section on steering (p. 90). After bearing away on to a run, changing the sail from one side to the other presents no difficulty provided you hold the mast at arms' length while the sail swings over the bow, and only then swiftly exchange hands.

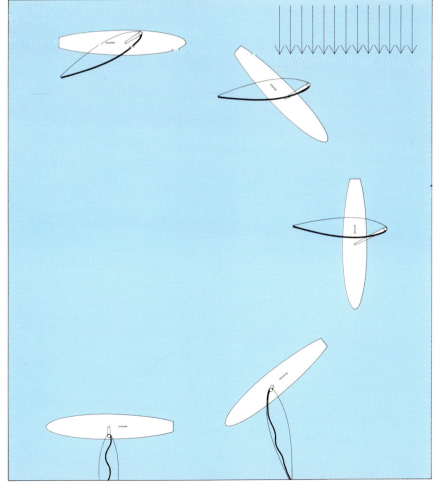

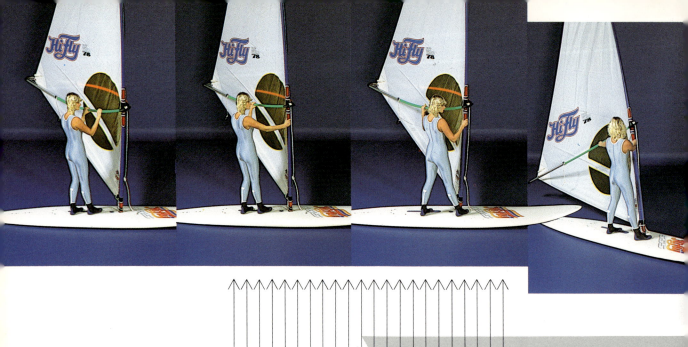

Tacking

Tacking can be broken down into two sections:
- A clear alteration of course by luffing up towards the wind.
- Turning in a semi-circle while swinging the sail round over the stern.

You prepare to tack while you are still sailing straight ahead by:
- Looking round to windward.
- Catching hold of the mast with your mast hand.
- Transferring your front foot forward of the mast.

The following movements should follow smoothly as you go about:
- Luff up until head to wind.
- Let go with your sail hand, step round forward of the mast, and change hands.
- Keep on turning until you are back in the basic position and can start off again.

Gybing

Gybing, like tacking, falls into two sections:
■ A clear alteration of course by bearing away from the wind on to a dead run.
■ Turning in a semi-circle while swinging the sail round over the bow, so as to continue sailing in the opposite direction on the other tack.

To gybe:
■ Look round to leeward.
■ Bear away until you are running.
■ Shift your front foot further back towards the stern, and then move your back foot further forward.
■ Grasp the mast with your mast hand.
■ Release the boom with your sail hand, and let the sail swing over the bow (don't bend your elbows!).
■ Change hands and continue to turn until you are back in the starting position on the other tack.
■ Start off again.

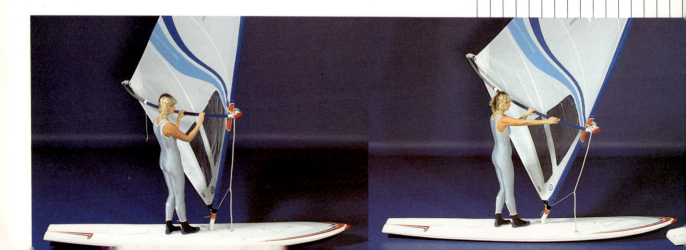

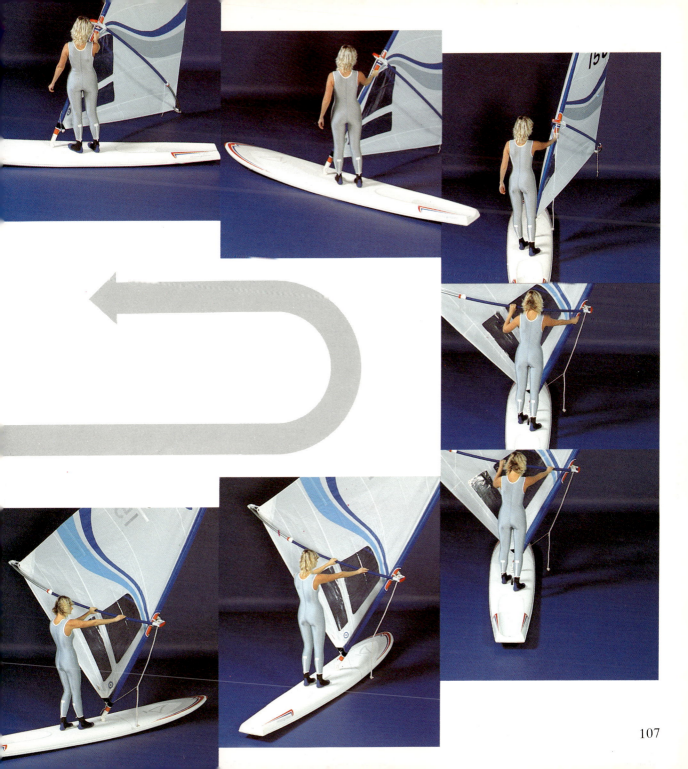

107

The wind you sail with

So far this book has only referred to the wind in general, but the wind you feel when on shore, for example when you are checking whether it is blowing towards or away from the land, is not the wind which you use to propel you. The latter wind differs in direction and strength from the 'normal' atmospheric wind.

It has already been explained (p. 98) that air consists of particles having mass and inertia. When an object, whether it be a tennis ball, a motor car or a sailboard, is moving faster or slower than the air around it, air resistance has to be overcome. You will be aware of this resistance when you are driving, for example, and will know that the wind which results from resistance arises whether there is a flat calm or a strong wind blowing. The speed of the wind caused by motion varies with the speed of the vehicle or vessel, but the direction of that wind is exactly opposite to the direction of motion.

What do these abstract facts mean to you as a boardsailor? Look at the figures below.

While you are standing in the basic position on the board with your sail shaking, you will only feel the atmospheric wind (boardsailor A). As soon as you gather way and start to move through the water, an additional wind arises due to board speed (boardsailor B).

Board speed and the atmospheric wind together result in the wind which is felt by boardsailor B as he sails, and which he uses for propulsion. This wind is called the relative wind because it arises from the relationship between the two types of wind, which themselves differ in direction and speed. The term 'true wind' is used frequently instead of atmospheric wind, just as 'apparent wind' is used instead of relative wind, but they are misleading terms because, when you are sailing on your board, you can really feel only relative wind.

Because the relative wind results from the combined effects of the two winds, with different directions and speeds, it will itself alter in speed and direction when:
- the direction of the atmospheric wind changes,
- the board alters course,
- the speed of the atmospheric wind changes,
- the speed of the board changes.

Whether separately or in combination, these four variable factors affect the direction and speed of the relative wind of the moment. Consequently you cannot expect to sail a longish distance on your board without a change in one or more of the contributing factors, and that will be allied to an alteration in the direction and speed of the relative wind.

In practice, then, it follows that you have to check constantly the angle of attack of your sail and to correct it, because your sail is fully efficient only when it is set at the correct angle to the airflow. This is why you must keep on testing whether you have trimmed the sail correctly, which you do by confirming that the luff is just not lifting.

Two values need to be looked at more closely: the direction in which the board sails, which defines the direction of the wind that arises from

The relative wind (W_R) is the result of the atmospheric wind (W_A) and the wind due to the board speed (W_S).

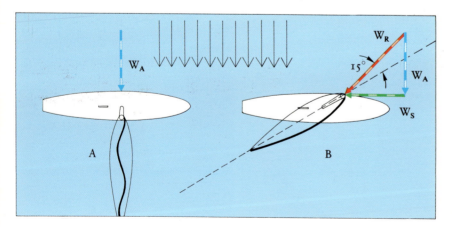

motion and the speed at which the board sails, which affects the speed of the relative wind.

The faster you sail, the farther forward will be the direction of the relative wind; furthermore its speed will be greater. Should you also be sailing close-hauled, the effect is that the relative wind will come from still further forward and its speed be still higher (see diagram). So it follows:

■ A boardsailor who is sailing very fast cannot point as close to the wind as one who is moving more slowly, but he can often reach an objective lying to windward just as, or even more, quickly (see p. 89).

■ In comparison with all other points of sailing you always have a lot of wind to cope with when hard on the wind. In spite of that, you sail relatively slowly when close-hauled because the sail has to be sheeted in so close on this point of sailing that the proportion of lateral force to total sail force is great whereas board speed is small.

Pressure on the sail is least when you are on a run, and on this point of sailing, which is directly downwind, 'air resistance' or board speed exactly opposes the atmospheric wind. Added to this is the fact that it is not the suction arising from air flowing over the cambered sail which provides propulsion (see Airflow over the sail, p. 98), but dynamic pressure. The fact that pressure on the sail is low when you are running can deceive you as to the real strength of the atmospheric wind, because the faster that you sail with the wind behind you, the more the speed of the wind you feel on the board decreases! Even when the trees are swaying on land you will imagine that the wind has eased or even dropped when you are on a run.

You must always bear this in mind when deciding whether to go out sailing when in an offshore wind; at first you will feel little pressure in the sail and the water will be calm (see p. 13), but you are bound to have to beat back to the shore, and in the meantime will probably have sailed into more open water where the atmospheric wind is blowing at full strength and where waves have formed. You will soon feel the effects; the waves make it hard to balance, even when you are raising the rig and starting, you will make little ground to windward, the pressure on your sail will increase, and the longer the distance you have to sail to get back, the more exhausted you become. Even if you are fit you may need help to return to the shore.

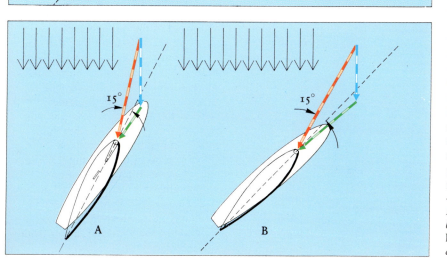

Above *The faster you sail, the nearer the bow will the wind direction be.*
Below *Because B is faster than A, B cannot point quite so high.*

109

Wind and Weather

Weather forecast

When boardsailing you are dependent on wind and weather to a large degree. It is easy to take a look at the weather by glancing out of the window, and what you see at that moment will help you to make important decisions: warm clothing, waterproofs, storm sail, anti-sunburn protection – yes or no? But the fact that is often ignored is that that glance out of the window gives sparse indication of the general weather situation, which can change in a remarkably short space of time.

It is, therefore, always worth while following weather maps and weather forecasts before a planned boardsailing weekend. With the help of information about the position of high and low pressure areas, and about sunshine and humidity, weather forecasters are able to make really reliable predictions as to cloud, temperature, precipitation and wind.

The coast in a Force 9 wind!

The additional help of satellite photography has improved the quality of weather prediction considerably.

Television weather forecasts give very little information about the development of weather, including the wind conditions expected, because these forecasts are aimed at the man in the street. It is difficult to make out what wind strength is expected from the very general terms used. A statement like 'light to moderate winds' has to be translated by you if you are to decide whether it will be worth your while spending the following day on the water. You will enjoy a flat calm as little as a storm with gusts of hurricane force.

If you decide that you are not satisifed with television or radio forecasts, you can telepone the special weather forecast centres which can be found in telephone directories and in leaflets issued by the Meteorological Office. However, the BBC Shipping Forecast on 200 kHz is very helpful, though it may not be accurate for a specific small area, especially on the coast, as opposed to well off shore.

Because of particular local conditions, the weather where you are boardsailing can differ considerably from the general weather situation, and it is therefore advisable always to obtain information about the local weather peculiarities wherever you are visiting, so that you are prepared for unpleasant surprises such as storms, wind shifts, thunder or fog. You can obtain some information from the harbour officer, where a forecast may be posted, or from local sailboard or sailing schools which will give you really reliable facts about weather development or possible dangers. Do not allow yourself to be led astray, however, blindly putting your trust in weather forecasts made by experts. Your own observation of weather and sky is irreplaceable.

For all that, it does no harm to have doubts not only about the official weather forecast but also about your own. You can guard against an unpleasant surprise if you take all possibilities into account and always remember to take a variety of suitable equipment and clothing with you. Your bag should contain the right gear for light or strong winds, and for high or low temperatures.

Wind and storm warnings

Gale warnings – Force 8 and over – are broadcast by the BBC on 200

A thunderstorm can build up in less than half an hour.

kHz and 'small craft' – Force 6 and over – warnings on some local radio stations. If a gale warning is in force, do not go boardsailing. Apart from endangering your life it is selfish to expect others to come to your rescue.

Weather forecasts and reports of 'present weather' are most widely available on radio and television.

Local harbour offices, sailing schools and sailing clubs often have meteorological bulletins posted.

Remember that forecasts are not infallible. Sometimes predicted strong winds will not materialise; at other times they will blow without warning. Out on the water the wind feels stronger than on the land or even on the beach.

Knowing what the wind strength will be does not mean that you will know how much pressure you will be supporting on the sail, because sail pressure results from wind speed. In a Force 4 wind, for example, wind speeds vary between 11 and 15 knots, and sail pressure varies with speed from about 19 to 39N/m² (0.003–0.006 lbf/sq in); pressure when air flows over a 6 sq m (65 sq ft) sail in a Force 4 wind, therefore, could be anywhere between 170N (38 lbf) at the lower limit and 350N (78 lbf) at the higher. You can control a 6 sq m sail reasonably well at the lower Force 4 limit, but not at the higher.

Broadly speaking, you can take it that wind pressure doubles every time the wind increases one force. If you take it that pressure on the sail in an average strength Force 1 wind is equal to 1 unit, pressure at Force 2 will be 2, at Force 3, 4, at Force 4, 8; even when the winds are Force 5, pressure will be 16 units. It is always sensible to see whether you can support your rig, with the sail extended, on shore before venturing forth.

Thunderstorms

When engaged in water sports, it is very important to recognise thunderstorms in good time so that you can take the necessary precautions. Dangerous hot weather thunderstorms can be recognised easily from these typical weather signs:

■ High air temperature and high humidity (oppressive and muggy).
■ Generally light winds.

Typical hot weather thunderstorm in high summer.

- Fair weather clouds (cumulus) which rapidly tower up to great heights.
- Increase in wind towards the thunderclouds.
- Thunder and lightning visible from a distance.

If you are surprised by a thunderstorm when out on the water, you could quickly find yourself unexpectedly in a dangerous situation. The first thundery gusts after a day of calms are extremely enticing but it would be utter foolishness to endanger yourself by going out to use them. There is not only a possibility of your being struck by lightning, but other problems may arise. The wind may suddenly increase to storm force and blow from the opposite direction, while rain or hail showers can limit visibility to such an extent that you do not know where you are on the water.

It is best and safest always to leave the water when a thunderstorm threatens, or at least to stay so close to the shore that you can reach it instantly. Should you, nevertheless, be surprised by a thunderstorm when on the water and be quite unable to return to land, remember the following rules:

- Drop your rig (the damp mast could act like a lightning conductor).
- Make yourself as small as possible, sitting on the board with feet tucked up to seat and arms around knees.
- Return to land only when the thunderstorm has passed.

Sailing in circles

Once you can tack and gybe, you have the basic skills needed for a typical test exercise on the water. This is simply to sail right round an island, or a buoy, or just to sail round in a circle. If you have so far managed to avoid gybing, now is the moment of truth.

Initially your circles will be really large, whether you want them to be so or not. When sailing circles you will soon discover your capabilities by comparing your skills with those of other boardsailors in the area. The closer and faster that you round the buoy, and the stronger the wind, the better!

Once you have mastered the art of turning circles, you will be sufficiently able to make your way to some more distant destination, such as a nearby bay or the other shore of a lake. For safety reasons, you

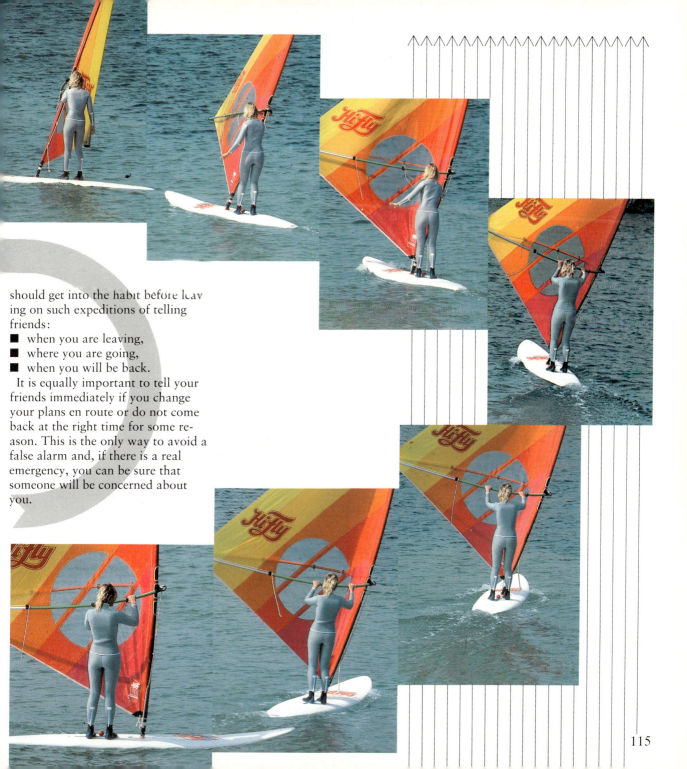

should get into the habit before leaving on such expeditions of telling friends:
- when you are leaving,
- where you are going,
- when you will be back.

It is equally important to tell your friends immediately if you change your plans en route or do not come back at the right time for some reason. This is the only way to avoid a false alarm and, if there is a real emergency, you can be sure that someone will be concerned about you.

When will I be an expert boardsailor?

It is very hard to define what an 'expert boardsailor' is. The reason for this is mainly that there are no clear-cut criteria, and that, too, is part of the attraction of boardsailing.

Thus, there is no such person as a boardsailor who *never* falls in the water, or who can keep sailing *whatever* the wind strength, or who can do every freestyle trick – and who knows anyway what tricks will be invented? Nor is there one who wins *every* race. Because of the unpredictability of natural forces, boardsailing ability is never absolute.

You very quickly establish your own ability by comparing yourself with others. You may be faster, point closer to the wind, reach the finish first, or be more knowledgeable. If you have no-one to compare yourself with because you sail alone or are in a class of your own, try to assess your own ability. You can check whether you have returned to the same spot from which you started, whether you have sailed a really tight circle round a buoy off shore, and whether you can still do this in winds of Force 3, 4, or 5 and more.

Do not worry if you fall into the water sometimes. That is all part of boardsailing and is nothing to be ashamed of. On the contrary, if you never fall in you are not really challenging yourself. When you fail to try out new things, you learn nothing; that is a well-known fact.

On the other hand, if you are permanently swimming in the water, something must be wrong. You could be making mistakes which you do not know how to correct yourself, or be over-pressing yourself. For example, the cause could be too much wind or too large a sail. In such a case do not delay but find your way to a windsurfing school; an experienced instructor will be happy to help you, and it is often only a small trick that cures the fault.

A school provides many opportunities for you to check your own ability. For some time there have been several certificates which confirm a person's boardsailing skills. The most widespread and best is the RYA boardsailing basic certificate. Further information can be obtained from the Royal Yachting Association, Woking, Surrey, England.

Basic certificate tests call for a certain minimum ability on the water, and compel you to have a good look, not only at your actions on the board and at the laws which govern water sports, but also at safety and environmental problems. Given future growth comparable to that of the last few years, it could soon barcly be possible to boardsail without instruction or some proof of ability. Purely to protect the people who are engaged in water sports from dangers which could arise through ignorance or lack of skill, water areas could be open only to those who can control their boards and have a knowledge of legal requirements.

Given mutually considerate, responsible behaviour and an awareness of nature and the environment (these are the most important points), any state intervention and control will be superfluous. You can remind yourself of your duty to help to avoid restriction of freedom in our sport by independent study and by your exemplary behaviour.

Where do I go from here?

Once you have mastered the art of sailing circles, your individual style will develop as you practise regularly. You will keep a look out for new waters and sailing areas and try to sail differently and rather better than 'Reservoir Harry'. You may decide to take up racing, or freestyle, or surf sailing after watching the specialists, whose tricks and techniques you can adopt yourself.

Racing

Skill and technique, plus knowledge and full use of the racing rules, decide who beats whom in a race. It does not have to be a major race such as Championships; even the most unimportant club races are exciting. Racing is not only very instructive, but provides endless discussion as to gear and tactics and how to sail still faster.

Freestyle

Freestyle ranges from playing around with board and sail while practising,

Racing.

to performing artistic and difficult tricks. Once you feel really sure on your board, try some simple exercises which will introduce you to freestyle. Try standing right forward or right aft on the board, and to sail kneeling, sitting or lying. This is not only fun but helps you to improve your balance and to develop sensitivity to the sail and to the reactions of the board. They are also essential requirements for strong wind sailing. Tricks such as spinning round (pirouette) when changing the sail from one side to the other, or turning round 360° on the board taking the sail with you (helicopter) are not too difficult in light winds. As a contrast, sailing on the rail to leeward of the sail is one of the most difficult tricks.

Sailing in surf

There is barely any risk in freestyle and racing, but when it comes to sailing in surf you should not venture out unless you are sure you can tack and gybe quickly, even in strong winds. You need to acquire the right techniques and skills in waters where you will not run into danger. Spectacular jumps are, of course, also possible using waves on inland waters provided the wind is strong enough. Once you have attempted this extreme branch of the sport, and have learnt to slalom in seas, as well as jumping, flying and landing safely in waves, you will have mastered a new dimension in boardsailing.

Left *Riding on the rail to leeward*
Right *Jumping in surf.*

Index

Aback 86, 87
Airflow 11, 98, 99
Allround board 22, 96
Allround funboard 22
Allround sail 56
Altering course 71, 74, 103ff
Angle of attack 97ff, 101
Atmospheric wind 108, 109

Back 86, 87
Basic position 63ff
Beam reach 88
Bear away 90ff
Beating 102, 109
Bird sanctuary 15
Boardsailing school 6, 8
Boardsailing restrictions 10, 72
Board steering 96
Board storage 40, 47, 48
Board-to-rig connection 18, 19, 24
Board transport 10, 28, 29, 30, 31
Boom 18, 19, 26, 56
Buoyancy aid 8, 27, 46

Catapult 94, 101
Centre of effort 95
Centre of lateral resistance 95
Chord of the sail 95, 97
Close-hauled 88, 89, 102, 109
Clothing 26, 27

Daggerboard 18, 19, 23, 26, 38, 52, 95
Direction of motion 80, 100
Displacement board 23
Distress signal 51
Downhaul 18, 97
Driving force 100, 101
Dry suit 27

Ease out 80, 81, 97
Emergency 51
Environment 10, 15ff, 117
Equipment 19, 20, 26, 27, 32
Exposure 26, 27, 46

Fin 18, 23, 40, 95
Foot 18

Foot positions 56, 62, 77, 94, 104, 106
Funboard 22

Going about 71, 100, 102, 114, 115, 109
GRP 24
Gybe 102ff, 71, 100, 102, 114, 115

Harden in 80, 81, 97

Inhaul 18, 19

Knots 34, 35, 41

Lateral force 100, 101
Lee 56, 57, 73, 99
Leech 18
Leeward 56, 57, 73, 99
Leeway 100, 101
Line of action 95
Local peculiarities 10, 11
Luff 18, 97
Luffing 90ff

Mast
Mast foot 18, 19
Mast hand 77, 78

Nature conservation 10, 15, 16, 17, 117
Neoprene 26, 27

Offshore wind 13, 46, 68
Onshore wind 13
On the wind 88, 89, 102, 109
Outhaul 18, 97
Overtaking 74, 99

Plane of the sail 90ff
Points of sailing 88, 89, 98, 108, 109
Polyester 24
Polyethylene 24
Polystyrene 24
Port tack 72

Racing 118, 119
Racing sail 20
Raising the rig 56ff
Rake 64, 65, 68
Reaching 88
Relative wind 108, 109
Rig 19, 42, 43, 47, 48

Rigging 36, 37
Right of way 71ff, 103
Roof load 28, 31
Roof rack 28, 29, 31, 30
Running 88, 89, 109

Sail 18, 20, 38, 39
Sail area 51, 95, 97
Sail cut 38, 95, 97
Sail hand 76, 78
Sailing circles 103, 114, 115
Sailing position 80, 81, 86, 87
Sail trim 97, 101
Sail tuning 38, 95, 97
Shallows 11
Sheet in 80, 81, 97
Sheet out 80, 81, 97
Shoes 27
Skin 24
Spare parts 24, 32
Spare rope 24, 32, 41, 52
Standing surface 44
Starboard tack 72
Start 76ff
Starting position 82, 83
Stopping 71, 86, 87, 93
Storm sail 111
Straps 30, 31
Strong winds 51, 78, 94, 96, 111
Surf 6, 46, 118, 119

Tacking 102, 109, 71, 100, 114, 115
Thunder 112, 113
Tide 11, 15
Towing 52, 53
Turning 60, 66ff, 96

Unrigging 42, 43, 50

Waves 13, 46, 56, 109
Weather 110ff
Weather helm 101
Wind due to board speed 108, 109
Wind force 22, 23, 111
Wind speed 111, 112
Wind strength 51, 78, 94, 96, 111, 112
Windward 56, 59, 73, 99